Advances in Computer Vision and Pattern Recognition

More information about this series at http://www.springer.com/series/4205

Massimo Tistarelli · Christophe Champod
Editors

Handbook of Biometrics for Forensic Science

Springer

Editors
Massimo Tistarelli
University of Sassari
Alghero, Sassari
Italy

Christophe Champod
University of Lausanne
Lausanne
Switzerland

ISSN 2191-6586 ISSN 2191-6594 (electronic)
Advances in Computer Vision and Pattern Recognition
ISBN 978-3-319-50671-5 ISBN 978-3-319-50673-9 (eBook)
DOI 10.1007/978-3-319-50673-9

Library of Congress Control Number: 2016959546

Printed on acid-free paper

This Springer imprint is published by Springer Nature
The registered company is Springer International Publishing AG
The registered company address is: Gewerbestrasse 11, 6330 Cham, Switzerland

Preface

Forensic Biometrics is a relatively novel discipline with a long-standing history. Even though this assertion may seem contradictory, it is true that biometric samples have been used in forensic examination since many decades. However, the systematic adoption of biometric technologies for criminal investigations and the incorporation in forensic processes is relatively new. In this regard, a considerable effort has been performed in the past 4 years by the European Union COST Action IC1106 "Integrating Biometrics and Forensics for the Digital Age."

The COST IC1106 research consortium is composed of over 40 members, research institutions, and forensic laboratories mainly from Europe and also from Australia, China, and USA. Aim of the Action has been to promote synergies between the biometrics recognition and the forensics science communities. This was achieved by means of innovative networking and scientific exchange. Most of the chapters making this edited volume are the outcome of this scientific collaboration.

Today's digital era is providing not only new computing solutions to assist forensics but also new threats and challenges, which cannot be solved with traditional approaches. These include identity-related scenarios such as attacks on security systems and the identification of abnormal/dangerous behaviors from remote cameras. New identification technologies and pattern recognition algorithms offer ways to provide proof of identity in these cases.

This book is the outcome of a strong new interdisciplinary community, which is establishing and disseminating good practice, and is stimulating novelty and interdisciplinarity in exploiting scientific possibilities.

While this trend deserves a growing attention, a strong impact is expected in many forensic scenarios, including identification at sensitive border crossing, analysis of video traces from surveillance cameras, and providing proof of evidence in court cases. This book presents a wide and in-depth view of the most advanced biometric technologies applied and purposively developed to forensic cases.

A multiview approach is presented to the reader, with each chapter being designed to cover a different subject written by authors from different research institutions, and the objective of covering the subject from different perspectives.

This comprehensive, innovative, state-of-the-art volume is designed to form and inform professionals, young researchers, and graduate students in the most advanced forensic biometrics technologies.

Alghero, Italy
June 2016

Massimo Tistarelli
Christophe Champod

Contents

Chapter 1
Biometric Technologies for Forensic Science and Policing: State of the Art

Christophe Champod and Massimo Tistarelli

Abstract In the last decades, biometric technologies have been applied in forensic investigations only to a limited extent of their possibilities. A number of factors have hindered the wider adoption of these technologies to operational scenarios. However, there have been a number of successful applications where biometric technologies were crucial to support investigation and to provide evidence in court. Given the great potential of biometric technologies for objective and quantitative evidence evaluation, it would be desirable to see a wider deployment of these technologies, in a standardized manner, among police forces and forensic institutes. In this chapter, after a review of the actual state of the art in forensic biometric systems, we try to identify some avenues to facilitate the application of advanced biometric technologies in forensic practice. Despite their impressive performance, some recent biometric technologies have never been applied to forensic evaluation. Other technologies will need adaptations to be ready for the forensic field. We postulate that there is a challenge to be faced with more advanced tools and testing on operational data. This will require a joint effort involving stakeholders and scientists from multiple disciplines as well as a greater involvement of forensic institutes and police forensic science departments.

1.1 A Short Historical Introduction and Forensic Context

For all tasks of authentication or identification in the context of investigations (civil or criminal), be it for investigative purposes or to be used as evidence in a court of law, biometric techniques play a key role. The difficulties associated with the

---

C. Champod (✉)
School of Criminal Justice, University of Lausanne, Lausanne, Switzerland
e-mail: christophe.champod@unil.ch

M. Tistarelli
PolComIng, Computer Vision Laboratory, University of Sassari,
Viale Mancini 5, 07041 Sassari, Italy
e-mail: tista@uniss.it

M. Tistarelli and C. Champod (eds.), *Handbook of Biometrics for Forensic Science*, Advances in Computer Vision and Pattern Recognition,
DOI 10.1007/978-3-319-50673-9_1

recognition of individuals on the basis of the memory of witnesses paved the way for recognition or identification techniques based on biometric features. As early as the turn of nineteenth century, Bertillon developed standardized descriptive techniques allowing the description and photographic documentation of faces [2]. Alongside, he implemented anthropometry, the standardized measurement of selected attributes of the human body [3]. That technique gained worldwide acceptance as a reliable method to help establishing identity when an unknown individual had to be confronted with a set of known persons that has been previously recorded. In the above historical context, the issue is the establishment of an identity of an unknown individual against a reference database of known individuals, either in verification mode (1 to 1) or in identification mode (1 to N). In addition, all measurements or photographed are acquired from living individuals in specified controlled conditions. Soon after Bertillon's anthropometry, the techniques taking advantage of fingerprints were introduced following the work by Galton, Faulds, Vucetich, and Henry (for a complete historical account refer to [19]). Fingerprints soon replaced anthropometry due to their ease of taking, classification and retrieval. But still, the technique is based on the pristine take of 10-print cards. Another major development, almost a side effect of the use of fingerprinting, is the capability to use marks, left inadvertently on objects potentially associated with criminal activities. These marks are left under uncontrolled conditions, may be distorted and smudged, visible or invisible to the naked eye. A range of techniques was developed to detect them. Even if marks are of significantly reduced quality compared to the quality of the controlled prints, they are an efficient mean for association with known prints. The first known cases of identification through the use of marks detected on crime scene are due to Vucetich in the 1892 Rojas case [16] and Bertillon investigated the 1902 Scheffer case [82]. In the first case, the mark was directly visible in blood, whereas in the second, Bertillon had to use white lead oxide powder to detect the marks on the glass pane. Through the years, the techniques used to visualize and enhance fingermarks (or other marks from friction ridge skin) progressed in terms of range of surfaces from which marks could successfully detected and in terms of sensitivity of the detection methods. Another key development was the organization of these methods in sequences starting from nondestructive optical methods towards more invasive but complementary physical or chemical techniques (see [15] for an overview of these methods).

Other biometric features left as marks have found some forensic applications since the early days before the major revolution i.e., DNA profiling. We note the use of barefoot impressions (either in insoles of shoes or recovered on scenes [95], earmarks collected from doors or windows [92], bitemarks [27] or facial images [84]). But of course, the first type of behavioral biometric used in forensic science is handwriting and signature whose usage goes back a few centuries [38].

It is in 1986 in the Pitchfork case that Alec Jeffreys introduced the possibility to analyze DNA in forensic science with a view to singularize individuals. It gave new possibilities to test for kinship and also identity based on biological material, fluids, and traces left on crime scenes (for an extensive overview of the field of DNA analysis refer to [10]). It was a major improvement compared to traditional serology testing that required substantial amount of material to obtain significant discrimination. Since its introduction in policing, DNA profiling gained in terms of sensitivity (capability to obtain a DNA profile from minute quantities of DNA, as low as a few picograms), and discrimination power. These progresses come with their lot of interpretative issues due to an increase of low level DNA mixtures with numerous contributors as it is now possible to obtain DNA from surface that have been on contact with multiple sources, as opposed to a large stain from on body fluid [11].

In forensic science, it all comes down to an attempt to compare material from unknown source(s) to material of known origin(s), in two typical scenarios, the first when the unknown material is taken under controlled conditions (such as for the identification of an unknown living individual) or under uncontrolled or unpredictable situations (such as for marks recovered from crime scenes or material from a dead body). This is one of the major contrasts between forensic science and other typical biometric systems used for access control or automatic border control. As soon as the gathered material is obtained under unconstrained conditions, the performance and the systems will suffer substantially. Another factor of complexity, that is shared with all biometric endeavor, is the within source variability, not only due to the acquisition conditions, but also to the source itself that may evolve to various degrees as a function of the age, time or intent.

Also, it is important to realize that the output of forensic work should not only be viewed in terms of provision of evaluative evidence in court, but it can take the form the production of information in the form of investigating leads. These two functions should be distinguished as the requirement for timeliness and reliability are different for both functions that we will refer to as “investigative” versus “evaluative” [44]. The use of DNA profiling will help to put this distinction into context. Most of national DNA databases are used to provide investigative leads in the form of the set of identifier for both known individuals and stains collected from investigated cases that have found correspondence (either in full, or partially suggesting close relatives) with a submitted unknown DNA profile. As such the information is not considered as evidence and will require being checked and interpreted by a DNA analyst. It is only the subsequent statement provided by the analyst (qualified with an appropriate measure of the weight to be attached to the findings) that will be presented as evidence in court. In some investigation, the fact that a DNA database has been used is not even disclosed in court (for example to avoid the court to be exposed to antecedents of the concerned individual). When a DNA database is searched, it is searched to minimize the risk of missed associations, as any association will be further challenged through the follow-up investigation and subsequent forensic analysis. However, when we ought to present the forensic findings in court as evaluative evidence, we wish to minimize the probability of a wrong association, or at the very least be transparent regarding this adverse probability.

1.2 Recent Developments of Biometric Technologies in Forensic Science

The development of automatic fingerprint identification systems (AFIS) has been steady since the mid-1960s [69]. Most of forensic systems were based on minutiae (either ridge endings or bifurcations of friction ridges) as the main features used for matching. From the outset of their development, these systems were not supposed to engage into any decision (as any other biometric system), but merely serve the purpose of speeding the search process when an fingerprint examiner is searching prints or marks against a database of already enrolled individuals or marks related to past cases. Indeed the decision as to whether the mark or the print belongs to a given known individual is left to the examiner that will apply the same process as if the suspect had been developed through another investigative means. The AFIS were used exclusively to bring appropriate candidates up in the list of candidates to consider one by one by the examiner as it represented a set of suspects to check against. The score, measuring the similarity between the query and the known is used only to rank the list of candidates. That being said, the accuracy of these systems is such that they allow bringing back the correct candidate in the considered list when a print or a mark is search among millions of cards and thousands of marks. These systems have progressed over the recent years to allow less interaction form the human examiner with the system. First, the images of high quality (often the case with good marks, well-taken prints) do not require much manual encoding but can benefit from auto-encoding algorithms that are very efficient. Second, when comparisons are undertaken on 2-print or 10-print cards, the accuracy allows setting automatic decision thresholds for identification. We are referring here about usage of AFIS systems in lights-out mode. The capacity to deal with marks (generally of lower quality than prints) is just a matter of time as the most advanced systems already allow to handle a fair amount of them (about 70%) in lights-out mode [65]. Third, the matching algorithms have progressed with the combined usage of both minutiae-based matching and image-based matching [41, 42].

The seminal work of Daugman [20–23] established the use of iris as an extremely strong biometric modality. It allows operating with extremely low probability of a false positive [33], used mainly for the identification of individual under supervised conditions (for immigration or border controls). For example, the wider system deployed for border control is in UAE. Iris is also one of the modalities retained alongside with fingerprints for the India's unique identification project *Aadhaar* (https://uidai.gov.in/). Progresses made in imaging sensors and at capturing irises at a distance allow using this modality in unconstrained conditions. Iris can be captured operationally with a 800 mm lens and a 850 nm infrared LED source at a standoff distance up to 8 m [93]. We can certainly for see applications in forensic science but they will be limited given the current state of technology to some constrained environments with cooperative individuals. We are far from an application in covert surveillance modes.

Forensic speaker recognition (FSR) has a long forensic tradition. It takes advantage of aural-perceptual (structured listening by trained phoneticians), auditory-instrumental (structured listening by trained phoneticians helped with specific measures such as the fundamental frequency and formant analysis), and also automatic methods inspired by the techniques used in biometrics [72]. The forensic practice varies a lot internationally [29]. The difficulties that forensic scientists face with FSR are due to the unpredictable nature of the technical conditions and background conditions under which the recordings are obtained. It is observed not so much for the controlled utterances, but systemically for the questioned recordings. It can be for example session mismatch (e.g., GSM telephone versus microphone), variations in the distance between the speakers and the microphone or the conditions of speech (stress, emotion, physical activities, overlapping talkers). All these imponderable variables impact on the accuracy of FSR [13] and it is wise to carefully assess the situations in which FSR can be reasonably undertaken [83].

The next biometric modality that has been developed and improved enormously in the recent years is face. Facial recognition systems have progressed to allow accurate facial recognition in controlled conditions such as automatic border controls or searches through database of mugshots. Needless to say that performance is affected by the size of the reference database and the age difference between the query facial image and the corresponding facial image in the gallery [32]. Moving from controlled conditions to unconstrained facial recognition is challenging as shown by Jain and colleagues [46, 48]. This is due to the general poorer quality of the images, variations in illumination, pose and occlusion caused by other objects and people. In today's policing, the number of facial images of non-identified individuals of interest is increasing fast. Their sources go from surveillance cameras, cameras from automated teller machine (ATM), personal devices, etc., Facial recognition, when the face is acquired under unconstrained conditions in terms of illumination or pose and with highly variable quality of images and background, is much more difficult but within the reach of current technology [4, 90] and certainly in the future. Some cases have been presented in the literature [53].

Recognition from police photo sketches is a niche application of biometry under mismatching conditions [52, 54]. It is an opportunity worth that every police force should be considering in serious cases.

Ear biometrics received attention as a means to improve on facial recognition under constrained conditions, apart from lightning [18, 40]. Performance has improved over the years to reach more than 95% accuracy [58]. To our knowledge, it has found limited applications in forensic science, mainly because the images of ears are not systematically acquired in adequate conditions during the booking process of individuals. Assessment of ear features while comparing two images of ears is currently carried out by forensic experts holistically on a case-by-case basis. This approach has shown limitations in terms of reliability [35]. The application of biometric techniques, in the sense of systematic and semi-automatic measurements on extracted features, on earmark collected from scenes and compared to earprints has led to interesting results as well [49, 50]. Reference earprints are not collected systematically upon arrest and hence it is foreseen that this modality will not be used in identification mode (1:N), but more frequently in verification mode (1:1).

Facial information may not be the only information available in images helping towards identification and often, in forensic conditions, the face is obscured, masked, or simply not visible. In these cases additional features such as scars, tattoos, vein patterns or knuckle patterns may be the only attributes helping associate an image with a given individual. Tattoo image recognition is certainly the closest to concrete operational forensic applications [61]. Knuckle patterns started as a classic biometric development taking advantage knuckles patterns taken under constrained conditions, patterns available on hands, easy to acquire in a noninvasive way [57, 96, 97]. Both major and (secondary) minor knuckle patterns can be used in conjunction and early data suggests that these patterns are stable over time [55, 59]. The modality is still in research stage but a steady increase in accuracy has been achieved [1]. We do foresee forensic avenues even under unconstrained conditions as shown in a recent paper [56]. However, the case will probably not be an identification mode, as databases of knuckle prints of persons of interest are not acquired on a systematic basis, but will more be a one-to-one comparison once an individual of interest comes to police notice. Dorsal hand veins patterns (that can also be visible on images of forensic interest) received also research attention, but mainly in constrained conditions with specific acquisition techniques taking advantage IR cameras (e.g., [75]). Stability of these vein patterns over time is not fully researched yet. At this stage, it is difficult to envisage an application under unconstrained conditions based on query images acquired under forensic conditions.

The use of scars (or other features such as nevi) to help identify persons has not received much attention in the biometric community, but scars were recorded as identifying features from the early days of forensic science. They received renewed interest in forensic science with the proliferation of images showing limited identifying features such as in cases of pedo-pornographic material where only hand on individual may be seen [8]. Assessing these features based only on expert judgment only has shown to be difficult [85] and researchers are striving to acquire systematic data to allow assign an appropriate weight to these comparisons [6, 7, 43].

Scars, marks, and tattoos (SMT) are features known as soft biometrics traits that include also characteristics such as height, weight, body geometry, gender, etc. [73, 79]. They can be typically described using human understandable labels and measurements. They can be obtained under unconstrained conditions (typically at a distance) and hence offer opportunities in surveillance applications [79, 89]. Soft biometric features can extend to attributes of individuals such as garments [45].

Moving back to more macro traits, gait analysis is receiving an increased attention in forensic science due to the proliferation of CCTV images [26, 60, 63]. Experts may use computer-assisted tools to carry out specific measurements on images or correct for distortion and perspective, but the recognition process is essentially carried out visually. Though, they have shown good ability to identify individuals using that process [5]. The biometric community also investigated the capabilities to detect and identify individuals based on gait features [74]. For a review of the latest development, refer to Makihara et al. [64]. In forensic science, one of the main challenge is related to the within source variability that may overlap the between sources variability, depending on the situation, the garments worn and fatigue [62]. Case-specific experiments are highly recommended.

1.3 Challenges

The challenges to deploy successfully biometric systems in forensic science have been described by a few authors already [24, 48, 68, 86]. For biometrics in general, we invite to refer to Jain et al. [47]. We will concentrate in this section on some key aspects.

One of the challenges posed by all forensic identification techniques described above lies in the fact that they are currently mostly based on the application of a holistic approach by trained experts. The decisions taken following the comparative examination are based on the informed judgment of the forensic analysts. Contrary to popular belief, all of these techniques, exception made of DNA profiling, do not find a systematic rooting in a statistical analysis, weighing the within-source variability against the between source variability. The case of fingerprint identification is covered in [15], but this state of affair runs across all the fields discussed above, apart from DNA. The paucity of systematic research in these areas has been highlighted by the 2009 report of the National Research Council [70].

Deploying biometric techniques in forensic science will require putting them in an adequate statistical reporting scheme. That scheme (see generally [14, 66]) is based on the concept of a likelihood ratio (LR) or Bayes factor. The LR is relative weighing of the probability to be assigned to findings given that the query and the known are from the same individual (hence allowing due consideration for the within source variability) against the probability of the findings given that the query and the known are from different individuals (hence giving due consideration for the between source variability in the relevant population). The LR provides the adequate measure of the weight to be assigned to the forensic observations and is recommended in Europe for reporting forensic evidence [94]. A specific guideline, also adopting a LR framework, has been developed for automatic and semi-automatic forensic speaker recognition as well [28].

Two challenges are then on the table when it comes to deploy biometric techniques in forensic science as evaluative evidence:

(1) If the technique is used to provide a piece of evidence as a standalone computerized method, then the research should demonstrate that the method is properly characterized by standardized measures of forensic efficiency. Here, the work carried out in speaker recognition [30, 78] and further extended to other forensic disciplines [76, 77] represents a major advancement. It is hoped

that the recently published guideline will pave the way forward towards more standardization [67];

(2) As mentioned before, forensic experts currently use most of the biometric techniques discussed above, applying their judgment informed training and experience developed through a large portfolio of cases. If biometric techniques bring new ways to assess the forensic findings, the combination of experts (traditional forensic and biometric experts) needs to be carefully researched. What will be the rules of engagement, how to deal with conflicting results, how to combine the respective information are not trivial questions and still have to find appropriate answers. We note some recent attempts with facial recognition [91] and hope to see more in future.

Not all biometric modalities used in forensic science will convey the same strength. For example, a fingermark displaying more than 12 minutiae deemed in correspondence with a print will on average bring a forensic weight (measured in terms of likelihood ratio) of above 1 billion [71], and so will a full 15-loci matching DNA profile [36]. In contrast, an earprints/marks correspondence will bring an average weight of 100 [50] or a few hundreds for voices under realistic forensic conditions [30]. It means that some biometric modalities will be well suited for both investigative and evaluative tasks, whereas others, such as face and ears, would be at first be used as investigative tools only. One of the challenges is to specify the appropriate framework of usage, so that the various stakeholders are very clear as how, when, and with what strength of information or evidence the modality will be used. An example on facial images is given in Dessimoz and Champod [25].

As 2D images and speech represent the main digital sensory data currently available to forensic scientists, we mainly concentrated on the processing of two-dimensional and one-dimensional signals. However, the development of 3D sensors will inevitably lead to an increased number of forensic cases where digital data will be available in 3D. On the other hand, researchers in biometric and computer vision technologies already demonstrated the feasibility of recognizing individuals from their 3D face shape, reconstructed from one or more 2D images. Inferring depth from one or more images has been studied for quite a long time in Computer Vision as *depth-from-X*, where "*X*" represents the visual cue exploited to infer the object 3D shape, i.e., stereo, motion, shading, etc. [31, 37, 81]. The main challenge has always been the accuracy required to reconstruct sufficient details in depth to allow the correct matching of individuals. The seminal work by Blanz and Vetter [9] introduced a novel parameterized model of face data, where the 3D facial appearance is directly related to both the face shape and the skin texture. The notable value of this research work is that the digital reconstruction of the 3D face shape is directly related to its 2D projection. In the last few years, several authors proposed different methods to reconstruct the 3D face shape from either a single image [34, 39, 51] or a sequence of images [17, 80]. The reconstructed face shape is generally used to produce a view-independent face image to match a reference face image captured at a given pose. This allows to reduce the errors due to the misalignment between the reference face, stored in a database, and the face captured from a given individual, either at a security check point or from a camera casually found on a crime scene. Attempts to directly use the reconstructed 3D face shape to perform recognition did not yet achieve the current state of the art in 3D face recognition [87].

In order to determine the feasibility of 3D face recognition, several 3D databases are now available to the scientific community. Many of them consist of high resolution scans of hundreds different individuals acquired with different poses and expressions (see http://www.face-rec.org/databases/ for an up to date list). This data allows to simulate real scenarios, where we need to take into account a high degree of variability. An algorithm devised to perform recognition from 3D face scans can be:

- completely automatic, operating in "lights out" mode as requiring human intervention may become prohibitive when dealing with thousands or millions of subjects;
- robust to changes in poses and facial expressions. In a real scenario, especially when dealing with images captured from surveillance cameras, it is impossible to select a given pose or facial expression.

Several algorithms for 3D face recognition have been proposed in the last decade. Recently an algorithm [12, 88] based on the extraction of facial features and the construction of a 3D signature manifold, based on 3D geometric invariants, demonstrated to be very effective in a number of very challenging test cases.

The results achieved so far, as well as other recent advances in biometrics research, do not ensure the applicability of the developed algorithms to forensic data, nor to solve every forensic case. However, given the great potential of these technologies in forensic investigations and for evidential evaluation, they are worth conducting further investigation to assess the applicability and performance which may be achieved on real forensic data.

1.4 Conclusions

As well exposed in this book, the identification of criminals from evidential traces or marks left on the crime scene has a long history in forensic science. As an example, in the late 50s the Federal Bureau of Investigations (FBI) in US regularly adopted fully manual procedures to match latent fingerprints with a large database of suspects on hundred thousands of print cards and started its work towards automation. Over the decades technology provided several instruments to automate the fingerprint matching process, also increasing the speed and accuracy. Since the late 90s, with the aid of the increased computation power and the reduced size of computing machines, the AFIS systems dramatically improved their performances allowing forensic expert to match and inspect hundreds of thousands fingerprint every day. As a result, the IAFIS (for Intergrated AFIS) currently working at FBI allows the forensic experts to match around 150,000 tenprints with a database of over 100 million subjects every day. The current TAR is 99.6% with 0.103% FAR. Such a workload would not be possible with human inspectors alone.

Fingerprint matching is just one example of many success stories where several technologies allowed to facilitate the work of forensic examiners, or even to make it possible to produce evidential statement in court. Over the past decades, other biometric technologies have been successfully applied including gait recognition and face image analysis. However, there are many other "biometric traits" and associated technologies, which can be successfully exploited as well.

Innovation does not influence the speed and accuracy of the identification process alone, but also the possibility to:

(1) handle different traces and their combination, including face pictures, action videos, speech, dna, iris, palmprints, footprints, skin marks, etc.
(2) perform a fully automated identification of suspects in "lights out" mode.

Current biometric technology is offering a plethora of solutions to handle many different traces or marks. However, not all state of the art technologies are currently deployed in forensic investigations. It is envisaged that more efforts are required to define new technological solutions which can be applied to given operational scenarios under purposively tailored protocols.

This chapter analyzed the current state of the art in biometric technologies trying to define a path forward to the innovation of currently exploited technologies in forensic investigations. This is just a start of a path which is further described in the following chapters and it is hoped to eventually enrich the knowledge and wider adoption of biometrics in forensic cases.

Acknowledgements This research is based upon work supported by the European Commission under the project COST IC1106 "Biometrics and Forensics for the Digital Age" and H2020 MSCA RISE 690907 "IDENTITY".

References

1. Amraoui M, Abouchabaka J, Aroussi ME (2014) Finger knuckle print recognition based on multi-instance fusion of local feature sets. In: 2014 international conference on multimedia computing and systems (ICMCS), 14–16 April 2014, pp 87–92. doi:10.1109/ICMCS.2014.6911188
2. Bertillon A (1890) La photographie judiciaire avec un appendice sur la classification et l'identification anthropométrique. Bibliothèque photographique. Gauthier-Villars et fils, Paris
3. Bertillon A (1893) Instructions signalétiques. Imprimerie administrative, Melun
4. Best-Rowden L, Han H, Otto C, Klare BF, Jain AK (2014) Unconstrained face recognition: identifying a person of interest from a media collection. IEEE Trans Inf Forensics Secur 9 (12):2144–2157. doi:10.1109/TIFS.2014.2359577
5. Birch I, Raymond L, Christou A, Fernando MA, Harrison N, Paul F (2013) The identification of individuals by observational gait analysis using closed circuit television footage. Sci Justice 53(3):339–342. doi:10.1016/j.scijus.2013.04.005
6. Black S, MacDonald-McMillan B, Mallett X (2014) The incidence of scarring on the dorsum of the hand. Int J Legal Med 128(3):545–553. doi:10.1007/s00414-013-0834-7

7. Black S, MacDonald-McMillan B, Mallett X, Rynn C, Jackson G (2014) The incidence and position of melanocytic nevi for the purposes of forensic image comparison. Int J Legal Med 128(3):535–543. doi:10.1007/s00414-013-0821-z
8. Black SM, Mallett X, Rynn C, Duffield N (2009) Forensic hand image comparison as an aid for paedophile investigations. Police Prof 184:21–24
9. Blanz V, Vetter T (1999) A morphable model for the synthesis of 3D faces. In: Proceedings of the 26th annual conference on computer graphics and interactive techniques (SIGGRAPH'99). ACM Press/Addison-Wesley Publishing Co., New York, NY, USA, pp 187–194. doi:http://dx.doi.org/10.1145/311535.311556
10. Butler JM (2010) Fundamentals of forensic DNA typing. Elsevier, Academic Press, Amsterdam
11. Butler JM (2015) Advanced topics in forensic DNA typing: interpretation. Elsevier, Academic Press, Amsterdam
12. Cadoni M, Bicego M, Grosso E (2009) 3D face recognition using joint differential invariants, advances in biometrics. In: Proceedings of the 3rd international conference on biometrics, ICB 2009, pp 279–288. doi:10.1007/978-3-642-01793-3_29
13. Campbell JP, Shen W, Campbell WM, Schwartz R, Bonastre JF, Matrouf D (2009) Forensic speaker recognition—a need for caution. IEEE Signal Process Mag 26(2):95–103. doi:10.1109/MSP.2008.931100
14. Champod C (2013) Overview and meaning of identification/individualization. In: Siegel JA, Saukko PJ (eds) Encyclopedia of forensic sciences. Academic Press, Waltham, pp 303–309. doi:10.1016/B978-0-12-382165-2.00197-5
15. Champod C, Lennard CJ, Margot PA, Stoilovic M (2016) Fingerprints and other ridge skin impressions, 2nd edn. CRC Press, Boca Raton
16. Chapman CL (1992) Dr. Juan Vucetich: his contribution to the science of fingerprints. J Forensic Ident 42(4):286–294
17. Choi J, Medioni G, Lin Y, Silva L, Pereira Bellon OR, Pamplona M, Faltemier TC (2010) 3D Face reconstruction using a single or multiple views. In: 20th international conference on pattern recognition ICPR 2010, Istanbul, Turkey, 23–26 Aug 2010, pp 3963–3966. doi:10.1109/ICPR.2010.963
18. Choras M (2009) Ear biometrics. In: Li SZ, Jain A (eds) Encyclopedia of biometrics. Springer, New York. doi:10.1007/978-0-387-73003-5_173
19. Cole S (2001) Suspect identities: a history of fingerprinting and criminal identification. Harvard University Press, Cambridge
20. Daugman J (2003) The importance of being random: statistical principles of iris recognition. Pattern Recognit 36(2):279–291. doi:10.1016/S0031-3203(02)00030-4
21. Daugman J (2006) Probing the uniqueness and randomness of IrisCodes: results from 200 billion iris pair comparisons. Proc IEEE 94(11):1927–1935. doi:10.1109/JPROC.2006.884092
22. Daugman J, Downing C (2001) Epigenetic randomness, complexity, and singularity of human iris patterns. Proc Royal Soc Biol Sci B 268:1737–1740. doi:10.1098/rspb.2001.1696
23. Daugman JG (1993) High confidence visual recognition of persons by a test of statistical independence. IEEE Trans Pattern Anal Mach Intell 15(11):1148–1161. doi:10.1109/34.244676
24. Dessimoz D, Champod C (2007) Linkages between biometrics and forensic science. In: Flynn PJ, Jain AK, Ross A (eds) Handbook of biometrics. Springer, New York, pp 425–459. doi:10.1007/978-0-387-71041-9_21
25. Dessimoz D, Champod C (2015) A dedicated framework for weak biometrics in forensic science for investigation and intelligence purposes: the case of facial information. Secur J (special issue on traceology) 29(4):603–617. doi:10.1057/sj.2015.32
26. DiMaggio JA, Vernon W (2011) Forensic gait analysis. In: Forensic podiatry: principles and methods. Humana Press, Totowa, NJ, pp 103–115. doi:10.1007/978-1-61737-976-5_6
27. Dorion RBJ (2005) Bitemark evidence. Forensic science. Marcel Dekker, New York

28. Drygajlo A, Jessen M, Gfroerer S, Wagner I, Vermeulen J, Niemi T (2016) Methodological Guidelines for Best Practice in Forensic Semiautomatic and Automatic Speaker Recognition. Verlag für Polizeiwissenshaften, Frankfurt
29. Gold E, Peter F (2011) International practices in forensic speaker comparison. Int J Speech Lang Law 18(2):293–307. doi:10.1558/ijsll.v18i2.293
30. Gonzalez-Rodriguez J, Rose P, Ramos D, Toledano DT, Ortega-Garcia J (2007) Emulating DNA: rigorous quantification of evidential weight in transparent and testable forensic speaker recognition. IEEE Trans Audio Speech Lang Process 15(7):2104–2115. doi:10.1109/TASL.2007.902747
31. Grimson WEL (1981) From images to surfaces: a computational study of the human early vision system. MIT Press
32. Grother PJ, Ngan ML (2014) Face recognition vendor test (FRVT)—performance of face identification algorithms, NIST interagency report 8009. National Institute for Standards and Technology, Gaithersburgh
33. Grother PJ, Quinn GW, Matey JR, Ngan ML, Salamon WJ, Fiumara GP, Watson CI (2012) IREX III: performance of iris identification algorithms, NIST interagency report 7836. National Institute of Standard and Technology, Gaithersburg
34. Hassner T (2013) Viewing real-world faces in 3D. In: International conference on computer vision (ICCV), Sydney, Australia, pp 3607–3614
35. Hoogstrate AJ, van den Heuvel C, Huyben E (2001) Ear identification based on surveillance camera images. Sci Justice 41(3):167–172. doi:10.1016/S1355-0306(01)71885-0
36. Hopwood AJ, Puch-Solis R, Tucker VC, Curran JM, Skerrett J, Pope S, Tully G (2012) Consideration of the probative value of single donor 15-plex STR profiles in UK populations and its presentation in UK courts. Sci Justice 52(3):185–190. doi:10.1016/j.scijus.2012.05.005
37. Horn BKP, Brooks MJ (eds) (1989) Shape from shading. MIT Press
38. Huber RA, Headrick AM (1999) Handwriting identification: facts and fundamentals. CRC Press, Boca Raton
39. Hu Y, Jiang D, Yan S, Zhang L (2004) Automatic 3D reconstruction for face recognition. In Proceedings of 6th IEEE international conference on automatic face and gesture recognition, FRGC 2004. IEEE, pp 843–848. doi:10.1109/AFGR.2004.1301639
40. Hurley DJ, Nixon MS (2009) Physical analogies for ear recognition. In: Li SZ, Jain A (eds) Encyclopedia of biometrics. Springer, New York. doi:10.1007/978-0-387-73003-5_172
41. Indovina M, Dvornychenko V, Hicklin RA, Kiebuzinski GI (2012) ELFT-EFS evaluation of latent fingerprint technologies: extended feature sets [Evaluation #2]. vol NISTIR 7859. National Institute of Standards and Technology, Gaithersburg
42. Indovina M, Hicklin RA, Kiebuzinski GI (2011) ELFT-EFS Evaluation of latent fingerprint technologies: extended feature [Sets Evaluation #1]. National Institute of Standards and Technology, Gaithersburg
43. Jackson G, Black S (2014) Use of data to inform expert evaluative opinion in the comparison of hand images—the importance of scars. Int J Legal Med 128(3):555–563. doi:10.1007/s00414-013-0828-5
44. Jackson G, Jones S, Booth G, Champod C, Evett IW (2006) The nature of forensic science opinion—a possible framework to guide thinking and practice in investigations and in court proceedings. Sci Justice 46(1):33–44. doi:10.1016/S1355-0306(06)71565-9
45. Jaha ES, Nixon MS (2014) Soft biometrics for subject identification using clothing attributes. In: 2014 IEEE international joint conference on biometrics (IJCB), Sept 29 2014–Oct 2 2014, pp 1–6. doi:10.1109/BTAS.2014.6996278
46. Jain AK, Klare B, Park U (2012) Face matching and retrieval in forensics applications. IEEE Multimed 19(1):20. doi:10.1109/MMUL.2012.4
47. Jain AK, Nandakumar K, Ross A (2016) 50 years of biometric research: accomplishments, challenges, and opportunities. Pattern Recog Lett 79:80–105. doi:10.1016/j.patrec.2015.12.013

48. Jain AK, Ross A (2015) Bridging the gap: from biometrics to forensics. Philos Trans Royal Soc Lond B: Biol Sci 370 (1674). doi:10.1098/rstb.2014.0254
49. Junod S, Champod C (2012) Earprint comparison: automated systems. In: Jamieson A, Moenssens AA (eds) Wiley encyclopedia of forensic science. John Wiley, Chichester. doi:10.1002/9780470061589.fsa1033
50. Junod S, Pasquier J, Champod C (2012) The development of an automatic recognition system for earmark and earprint comparisons. Forensic Sci Int 222(1–3):170–178. doi:10.1016/j.forsciint.2012.05.021
51. Kemelmacher-Shlizerman I, Basri R (2011) 3D face reconstruction from a single image using a single reference face shape. IEEE TPAMI 33(2):394–405. doi:10.1109/TPAMI.2010.63
52. Klare B, Li Z, Jain AK (2011) Matching forensic sketches to mug shot photos. IEEE Trans Pattern Anal Mach Intell 33(3):639–646. doi:10.1109/TPAMI.2010.180
53. Klontz JC, Jain AK (2013) A case study of automated face recognition: the Boston marathon bombings suspects. IEEE Comput 46(11):91–94 . doi:10.1109/MC.2013.377
54. Klum S, Han H, Jain AK, Klare B (2013) Sketch based face recognition: forensic vs. composite sketches. In: 2013 international conference on biometrics (ICB), 4–7 June 2013, pp 1–8. doi:10.1109/ICB.2013.6612993
55. Kumar A (2012) Can we use minor finger knuckle images to identify humans? In: 2012 IEEE fifth international conference on biometrics: theory, applications and systems (BTAS), 23–27 Sept 2012, pp 55–60. doi:10.1109/BTAS.2012.6374558
56. Kumar A (2014) Importance of being unique from finger dorsal patterns: exploring minor finger knuckle patterns in verifying human identities. IEEE Trans Inf Forensics Secur 9 (8):1288–1298. doi:10.1109/TIFS.2014.2328869
57. Kumar A, Ravikanth C (2009) Personal authentication using finger knuckle surface. IEEE Trans Inf Forensics Secur 4(1):98–109. doi:10.1109/TIFS.2008.2011089
58. Kumar A, Wu C (2012) Automated human identification using ear imaging. Pattern Recognit 45(3):956–968. doi:10.1016/j.patcog.2011.06.005
59. Kumar A, Xu Z (2014) Can we use second minor finger knuckle patterns to identify humans? In: 2014 IEEE conference on computer vision and pattern recognition workshops, 23–28 June 2014, pp 106–112. doi:10.1109/CVPRW.2014.21
60. Larsen PK, Simonsen EB, Lynnerup N (2008) Gait analysis in forensic medicine. J Forensic Sci 53(5):1149–1153. doi:10.1111/j.1556-4029.2008.00807.x
61. Lee J, Jin R, Jain AJ, Tong W (2012) Image retrieval in forensics: tattoo image database application. IEEE Multimed 19(1):40–49. doi:10.1109/MMUL.2011.59
62. Ludwig O, Dillinger S, Marschall F (2016) Intra-individual gait pattern variability in specific situations: Implications for forensic gait analysis. Forensic Sci Int 264:15–23. doi:10.1016/j.forsciint.2016.02.043
63. Lynnerup N, Vedel J (2005) Person identification by gait analysis and photogrammetr. J Forensic Sci 50(1):1–7. doi:10.1520/JFS2004054
64. Makihara Y, Matovski DS, Nixon MS, Carter JN, Yagi Y (2015) Gait recognition: databases, representations, and applications. Wiley Encyclopedia of Electrical and Electronics Engineering, pp 1–15. doi:10.1002/047134608X.W8261
65. Meagher S, Dvornychenko V, Garris M (2014) Characterization of latent print "lights-out" modes for automated fingerprint identification systems. J Forensic Ident 64(3):255–284
66. Meuwly D (2006) Forensic individualisation from biometric data. Sci Justice 46(4):205–213. doi:10.1016/S1355-0306(06)71600-8
67. Meuwly D, Ramos D, Haraksim R (to appear) A guideline for the validation of likelihood ratio methods used for forensic evidence evaluation. Forensic Sci Int. doi:10.1016/j.forsciint.2016.03.048
68. Meuwly D, Veldhuis R (2012) Forensic biometrics: from two communities to one discipline. In: Proceedings of the international conference of the biometrics special interest group (BIOSIG), 2012 BIOSIG, 6–7 Sept 2012, pp 1–12

69. Moses K (2011) Chapter 6: Automatic fingerprint identification systems (AFIS). In: McRoberts A (ed) The fingerprint sourcebook. National Institute of Justice, Washington DC, pp 6-1–6-33
70. National Research Council (2009) Strengthening forensic science in the United States: a path forward. The National Academies Press, Washington, DC
71. Neumann C, Evett IW, Skerrett J (2012) Quantifying the weight of evidence from a forensic fingerprint comparison: a new paradigm. J Roy Stat Soc Ser A (Stat Soc) 175(Part 2):371–415 (with discussion)
72. Neustein A, Patil HA (eds) (2012) Forensic speaker recognition. Springer, New York. doi:10.1007/978-1-4614-0263-3
73. Nixon MS, Correia PL, Nasrollahi K, Moeslund TB, Hadid A, Tistarelli M (2015) On soft biometrics. Pattern Recog Lett 68(Part 2):218–230. doi:10.1016/j.patrec.2015.08.006
74. Nixon MS, Tan TN, Chellappa R (2006) Human identification based on gait. International series on biometrics. Springer, New York. doi:10.1007/978-0-387-29488-9
75. Raghavendra R, Surbiryala J, Busch C (2015) Hand dorsal vein recognition: sensor, algorithms and evaluation. In: 2015 IEEE international conference on imaging systems and techniques (IST), 16–18 Sept. 2015, pp 1–6. doi:10.1109/IST.2015.7294557
76. Ramos D, Gonzalez-Rodriguez J (2013) Reliable support: measuring calibration of likelihood ratios. Forensic Sci Int 230(1–3):156–169. doi:10.1016/j.forsciint.2013.04.014
77. Ramos D, Gonzalez-Rodriguez J, Zadora G, Aitken C (2013) Information-theoretical assessment of the performance of likelihood ratio computation methods. J Forensic Sci 58 (6):1503–1518. doi:10.1111/1556-4029.12233
78. Ramos-Castro D, Gonzalez-Rodriguez J, Ortega-Garcia J (2006) Likelihood ratio calibration in a transparent and testable forensic speaker recognition framework. In: Speaker and language recognition workshop, 2006. IEEE Odyssey 2006: The, 28–30 June 2006, pp 1–8. doi:10.1109/ODYSSEY.2006.248088
79. Reid DA, Samangooei S, Chen C, Nixon M, Ross A (2013) Soft biometrics for surveillance: an overview. In: Govindaraju V, Rao CR (eds) Handbook of statistics, vol 31. Elsevier, North Holland, Amsterdam, pp 327–352. doi:10.1016/B978-0-44-453859-8.00013-8
80. Roth J, Tong Y, Liu X (2015) Unconstrained 3D face reconstruction. In: The IEEE conference on computer vision and pattern recognition (CVPR), pp 2606–2615. doi:10.1109/CVPR.2015.7298876
81. Sandini G, Tistarelli M (1990) Active tracking strategy for monocular depth inference over multiple frames. IEEE Trans PAMI PAMI-11(12):13–27. doi:10.1109/34.41380
82. Sannié C (1950) Alphonse Bertillon et la dactyloscopie. L'affaire Scheffer. Revue internationale de police criminelle 5(41):255–262
83. Schwartz R, Campbell JP, Shen W (2011) When to punt on speaker comparison? J Acoust Soc Am 130(4):2547. doi:10.1121/1.3655180
84. Spaun NA (2011) Face recognition in forensic science. In: Li SZ, Jain AK (eds) Handbook of face recognition. Springer International Publishing, pp 655–670. doi:10.1007/978-0-85729-932-1_26
85. Stevenage SV, Walpole C, Neil GJ, Black SM (2015) Testing the reliability of hands and ears as biometrics: the importance of viewpoint. Psychol Res 79(6):989–999. doi:10.1007/s00426-014-0625-x
86. Tistarelli M, Grosso E, Meuwly D (2014) Biometrics in forensic science: challenges, lessons and new technologies. In: Cantoni V, Dimov D, Tistarelli M (eds) Biometric authentication: first international workshop, BIOMET 2014, Sofia, Bulgaria, June 23–24, 2014. Revised Selected Papers. Springer International Publishing, Cham, pp 153–164. doi:10.1007/978-3-319-13386-7_12
87. Tistarelli M, Cadoni M, Lagorio A (2016) Matching reconstructed 3D face shapes. Personal communication
88. Tistarelli M, Cadoni M, Lagorio A, Grosso E (2016) Blending 2D and 3D face recognition. In: Bourlai T (ed) Face recognition across the imaging spectrum. Springer International Publisher, pp 305–331. doi:10.1007/978-3-319-28501-6_13

89. Tome P, Fierrez J, Vera-Rodriguez R, Nixon MS (2014) Soft biometrics and their application in person recognition at a distance. IEEE Trans Inf Forensics Secur 9(3):464–475. doi:10.1109/TIFS.2014.2299975
90. Tome P, Fierrez J, Vera-Rodriguez R, Ramos D (2013) Identification using face regions: application and assessment in forensic scenarios. Forensic Sci Int 233(1–3):75–83. doi:10.1016/j.forsciint.2013.08.020
91. Tome P, Vera-Rodriguez R, Fierrez J, Ortega-Garcia J (2015) Facial soft biometric features for forensic face recognition. Forensic Sci Int 257:271–284. doi:10.1016/j.forsciint.2015.09.002
92. Van der Lugt C (2001) Earprint identification. Elsevier's-Gravenhage
93. Venugopalan S, Prasad U, Harun K, Neblett K, Toomey D, Heyman J, Savvides M (2011) Long range iris acquisition system for stationary and mobile subjects. In: 2011 international joint conference on biometrics (IJCB), 11–13 Oct 2011, pp 1–8. doi:10.1109/IJCB.2011.6117484
94. Willis SM et al (2015) ENFSI guideline for evaluative reporting in forensic science. European Network of Forensic Science Institutes, Dublin. http://enfsi.eu/sites/default/files/documents/external_publications/m1_guideline.pdf
95. Yamashita BA, Kennedy RB (2009) Forensic barefoot comparison. In: Li SZ, Jain A (eds) Encyclopedia of biometrics. Springer, New York. doi:10.1007/978-0-387-73003-5_181
96. Zhang L, Zhang L, Zhang D, Zhu H (2010) Online finger-knuckle-print verification for personal authentication. Pattern Recognit 43(7):1571–2560. doi:10.1016/j.patcog.2010.01.020
97. Zhang L, Zhang L, Zhang D, Zhu H (2011) Ensemble of local and global information for finger–knuckle-print recognition. Pattern Recognit 44(9):1990–1998. doi:10.1016/j.patcog.2010.06.007

Part I
Analysis of Fingerprints and Fingermarks

Chapter 2
Capture and Analysis of Latent Marks

Mario Hildebrandt, Jana Dittmann and Claus Vielhauer

Abstract The capture and analysis of latent marks in forensics has a history of over a century. The focus of this chapter is on the marks formed by fingerprint patterns. The process starts with the detection and acquisition of the marks using different physical, chemical and optical means. Additionally, experimental approaches for determining the age or exploiting the finger mark persistency, as well as digital enhancement techniques are described. Afterward, the analysis is performed in four steps. Here, features on three different levels are determined, evaluated and compared between two fingerprint patterns. The result of such a comparison, also known as dactyloscopy, is nowadays either an identification, exclusion or inconclusive. In the future those outcomes might be replaced with a likelihood ratio which allows for expressing uncertainties on a statistical foundation. In order to use new methods in court, particular requirements must be assessed. For this, the Daubert challenge, which includes the assessment of several factors by a judge, is briefly summarized.

M. Hildebrandt (✉) · J. Dittmann · C. Vielhauer
Department of Computer Science, Research Group Multimedia and Security,
Otto-von-Guericke-University of Magdeburg, PO Box 4120, 39016 Magdeburg, Germany
e-mail: mario.hildebrandt@iti.cs.uni-magdeburg.de

J. Dittmann
e-mail: jana.dittmann@iti.cs.uni-magdeburg.de

C. Vielhauer
e-mail: claus.vielhauer@iti.cs.uni-magdeburg.de

J. Dittmann
The University of Buckingham, Buckingham, UK

C. Vielhauer
Department of Informatics & Media, Brandenburg University of Applied Sciences,
PO Box 2132, 14737 Brandenburg, Germany

M. Tistarelli and C. Champod (eds.), *Handbook of Biometrics for Forensic Science*, Advances in Computer Vision and Pattern Recognition,
DOI 10.1007/978-3-319-50673-9_2

2.1 Introduction

The acquisition and analysis of latent marks from the perspective of fingerprints is one of the oldest disciplines in forensic science which also paved the way for the utilization of the fingerprint as a biometric modality in a manifold of applications. Of course there are known differences in both domains such as briefly summarized as follows:

(1) The fingerprint trace (finger mark) is formed by human secretions (e.g., invisible human sweat) left by a finger touching a surface (also called latent mark) or caused due to the removable, adherent or deformable nature of the a surface property (such as other liquids on the surface, e.g., visible blood or ink, surface dust—also called often patent mark, or ductile and plastic surface behavior also called plastic mark (see [1, pp. 105–106]). Depending on the visibility of the mark, the fingerprint characteristics might be invisible to the human eye. As the presence and location of fingerprint traces is not known a priori in forensics, the marks need to be searched for and found (detected) at first. Due to the small size of the marks and very often its invisible (latent) nature on the surface, the search needs to include mechanisms to turn the mark visible and/or accessible for further acquisition techniques. This can be done either by using a physical or chemical treatment, see details in the third section, allowing for acquiring camera photos, or with contact-less methods which exploit properties of the residue using special sensory such as optical, nanometer range sensing or special lighting conditions (UV or infrared, see also in the following forth section) further combined with an additional so-called digital treatment. Contact-less, non-destructive approaches are of course very valuable allowing trace processing several times without altering the trace itself.

(2) For trace detection as well as for analysis after acquisition the trace needs to be separated or segmented from the surface to see if the finger mark contains a sufficient number and quality of forensically relevant characteristics (see Sect. 2.2).

(3) The analysis is usually performed by a forensic expert (called dactyloscopy expert or latent print examiner) supported with further means (microscopes, digital processing, etc.) as described in Sect. 2.5.

(4) Additional forensic challenges which occur in the case work are for example:

(a) **overlapping marks**: Detection of overlapping marks, determination of the kind of overlapping traces (e.g., when other traces such as fibers are expected) and/or number of overlapping marks, separation of the marks with its quality assessment (see e.g. [2, 3]).
(b) **trace age estimation**: Determination of absolute or relative time the trace was left at the crime scene, the trace age is valuable to exclude or include traces which are, e.g., older or younger at time of interest, as summarized in [4].

(c) **forgery detection**: As known and discussed in several publications such as Harper [5] or Wertheim [6] and more recently [7], crime scene trace forgeries are present and need to be detected. In [8] for example several artificial sweat printed fingerprints and corresponding forgery detection approaches are summarized and benchmarked.

In comparison to the forensic case, in the biometric case, the fingerprint is explicitly and intentionally presented to the biometric sensory, producing a so-called exemplar fingerprint. Therefore, the detection from the forensic case (1) is limited here to searching and locating the fingerprint in a particular limited sized sensor region. In respect to (2), depending on the kind of biometric sensory used, the surface separation and segmentation is fixed and well defined. The analysis from (3) is usually performed by a biometric algorithm.

In respect to further challenges (4):

(a) overlapping marks occur in case of contact-based sensing, where remaining secretions from a preceding touch remains on the sensory. Here it might be valuable that the sensory detects that there are disturbances and is doing or requesting a cleaning as solution in this case.

In biometrics, the mark age (trace age (4)(b)) can be determined explicitly during sensor acquisition with the sensor time. For both domains, the age of the subject might be also of interest, see for example discussion about challenges caused by aging of fingerprint in [9].

Forgery detection (c) is also relevant for biometric applications. The kind of forgeries differs in respect to the time and means, such as artificial sweat printings cannot be easily placed in from of a biometric sensory to forge it, but 3D fingers of course can be produced to forge both domains. Liveness detection or presentation attack detection is therefore a relevant feature in the biometric domain, while in forensic domain even marks and prints from dead subjects might be of interest in order to link them to a crime or to identify corpses.

In the forensic case the finger mark is evaluated in order to determine whether the mark's characteristics belong to a particular known subject by comparing it either with exemplar prints taken under controlled conditions directly from the subject or with other latent marks found at crime scenes where the subject's identity is not known, yet. Nowadays, potential outcomes of this comparison are an inconclusive result if an insufficient number of usable features is present and an exclusion for sufficiently different patterns or an identification if the mark has a sufficient number of characteristics in common with the pattern is has been compared to. In the future alternative measure likelihood ratios might be used (see e.g. [10]). In the biometric case, a verification or identification is performed by using samples from a template database which has to be created in advance in the enrollment stage (called enrollment sample(s), reference(s), template(s)). Known error rates are the false acceptance rate (FAR, also known as type 1 error) and false rejection rate (FRR, also known as type 2 error) as well as the failure to enroll rate (FTE) and failure to acquire rates (FTA), additionally the equal error rate (EER) is used to describe the performance of a biometric system [11, pp. 6–12].

An additional challenge here is the sensor dependency of template and test samples and cross-sensor evaluations are of interest (see e.g. [12]).

This chapter provides a brief overview over the state of the art of the acquisition and analysis of latent marks. In line with the literature, e.g. [1], the term finger mark is used for the latent trace at the crime scene, whereas the term fingerprint is used for an exemplar print captured directly from the finger e.g. within a biometric system. The term fingerprint pattern is used for the pattern of both, fingerprints as well as finger marks.

The remainder of this chapter is structured as follows: Sect. 2.2 summarizes the fingerprint characteristics as a foundation for the comparison. The current state of the art regarding conventional latent mark acquisition techniques is discussed in Sect. 2.3. An overview of contact-less, non-destructive acquisition techniques is presented in Sect. 2.4. In Sect. 2.5 the finger mark analysis process is discussed. Afterward, particular legal challenges for new techniques are discussed in Sect. 2.6. Subsequently, the chapter is summarized in Sect. 2.7.

2.2 Fingerprint Characteristics

The foundations for the analysis of fingerprints and marks are primarily established by Johann C. A. Mayer [13], Johann E. Purkinje [14], William Herschel [15], Henry Faulds [16], Francis Galton [17], Edward Henry [18], Edmond Locard and Salil Chatterjee whereas the usage of fingerprints in general dates back several centuries, see e.g. [19] for historical timeline of forensic sciences.

Mayer [13, pp. 5–6] described the uniqueness of the fingerprint pattern for the first time in his explanation of the second copper-plate: "*Although the wrinkles of two humans are never coincide with each other, nevertheless some humans have more similarities whereas others seem to differ more in their visual appearance. However, the peculiarities of all arrangement are similarly formed.*"

Purkinje [14] describes a classification of nine global patterns of the fingerprint: simple arch, tented arch, oblique stripe, oblique loop, almond, spiral, ellipse, circle and double whorl. Starting in 1858, Herschel [15] utilized the fingerprint patterns as a means of identification in India. The uniqueness of the skin furrows is also described by Henry Faulds [16] based on experiments with fingerprints from monkeys and humans. It is also one of the first public articles considering the usage of fingerprints for performing individualization at crime scenes.

Galton [17] describes different kinds of arches, loops and whorls as global patterns, as well as minutiae points and pores. He also discusses the evidential value of fingerprints, indexing methods and personal identification. Galton also performed experiments on the fingerprint pattern persistency.

Henry [18] developed a classification system for fingerprints in collaboration with Galton. He differentiates between the delta and core points of the global level one pattern. For his primary classification he differentiates between loops (including arches) and whorls for five pairs of two fingers [18, pp. 69–75].

Locard established the first rules towards a minimum number of minutiae points which are necessary for identification (see e.g. [20]) in 1914. Furthermore, he established the science of the poroscopy [21] in 1912. However, his most important contribution to forensic sciences is probably the formulation of his exchange principle (see e.g. [22, p. 44]), which is the foundation for many other forensic disciplines as well. It basically states that every offender inevitably leaves traces at the scene of crime and takes traces from it with him as well.

Chatterjee described the analysis of the edges of the ridge lines, known as edgeoscopy [21], in 1962.

Nowadays, as known, three different levels of features are used within the scope of fingerprints [1, pp. 15–20]. The first level describes the global pattern which is visible on the fingertip even to the bare eye. The second level describes local characteristics, known as minutiae points. Those particular features are primarily used for matching fingerprints. The third level of features describes microscopic details such as pores or the edges of papillary lines. In the following the characteristics for each feature level are described.

The first level of fingerprint features has already been used e.g. by Galton [17] and Henry [18] for their classification systems. In particular, usually the five different global pattern types left loop, right loop, whorl, (plain) arch, tented arch are used.

In forensic investigations those patterns can be used for a quick exclusion. However, a matching level 1 pattern is insufficient for a verification or identification of individuals. Besides their different visual appearance the patterns share some properties regarding the number of core and delta points. The delta points are characterized by a triangular-shaped region within the ridge flow. Thus, the ridge flow has three different orientations within close proximity of this point. The core point is a point where the ridge orientation significantly changes or, in other words, a point with a non-continuous ridge flow in its neighborhood.

An arch has no core and delta points at all. Tented arches, left loops and right loops have one core and one delta point. Whorls have two core points and two delta points.

The level 2 patterns describe local characteristics of the ridge flow. The most common level 2 features are called minutiae points. Other features include warts, scars, creases, wrinkles, incipient ridges and subsidiary ridges [1, p. 17]. The two most common minutiae types are ridge endings (a termination of the papillary line) and bifurcations (a splitting point of one papillary line into two ridges) as illustrated in Fig. 2.1.

Usually four types of information are stored for each minutiae point: the x and y coordinates, the minutiae type and the orientation of the minutiae. Depending on the utilized format the origin of the coordinate system can be in the lower left or upper left corner of the image. Furthermore, the coordinates can be stored as pixel values or in metric units. Especially the latter has the advantage of achieving a resolution independent template. The orientation of the minutiae is determined as depicted in Fig. 2.2.

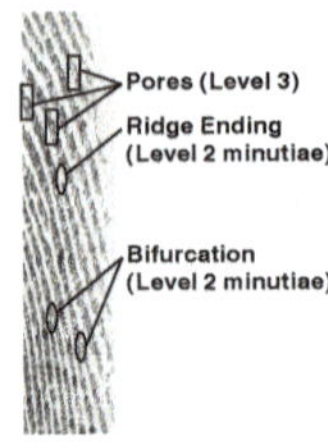

Fig. 2.1 Illustration of minutiae and pores (re-sketched)

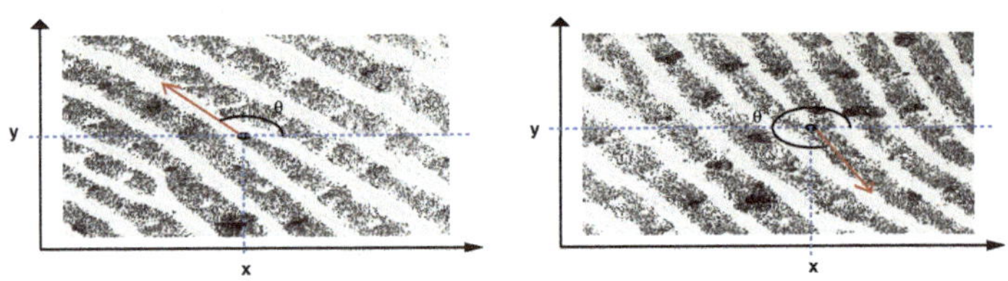

Fig. 2.2 Minutiae orientation: ridge ending (*left*) and bifurcation (*right*) (re-sketched)

For ridge endings the angle of the minutiae is determined by measuring the angle θ between the perpendicular line through the y coordinate and the prolonged ridge line. For bifurcations the angle is determined between the perpendicular line through the y coordinate and the prolonged valley between the two ridges.

On the third level of features, primarily small details are investigated. Such features include pores as illustrated in Fig. 2.1 and edges of the ridges. The pores are formed by the sweat glands on the ridges. Due to their nature, a high acquisition resolution of at least 1000 ppi is required in order to be able to extract such features reliably. Common biometric systems usually take no advantage of those features, see e.g. [23]. In contrast to that, especially for partial finger marks, in forensics such features can make a difference between an inconclusive comparison and an exclusion or identification of the mark.

2.3 Conventional Latent Mark Acquisition Techniques

Several latent mark detection and acquisition techniques exist and are applied in daily police work. Such methods are usually necessary to render the invisible residue from the fingertip visible. Some of those methods are also combined with special illumination techniques for further contrast enhancement.

The detection techniques are usually divided into methods for non-porous and porous substrates. On non-porous substrates the residue resides on top of the object with the finger mark. In contrast to that, the residue is absorbed over time into porous substrates. A detailed description of the multitude of detection techniques is provided in [1, pp. 111–173] and [24]. Due to the nature of these techniques the latent mark is inevitably altered in terms of its chemical composition during the processing. Therefore, the forensic laboratories implement the ISO 17025 Standard to produce consistent results [24]. In the following, the most commonly applied known techniques for the latent mark development such as powdering, cyanoacrylate fuming, vacuum metal deposition, ninhydrin spraying, physical developer and multimetal deposition are summarized.

The oldest detection technique for smooth non-porous substrates is the powdering of the finger marks, see e.g. [1, pp. 136–137]. During this physical treatment powder particles are applied to the mark using brushes in order to detect the mark. The particles adhere to the greasy, sticky or humid substances in the residue and thus, render the mark visible. Afterward, the mark can be photographed and/or lifted using adhesive tape or gel lifters. Due to the low cost and low requirements regarding equipment and special training, this technique is still the most commonly applied method for latent marks detection at crime scenes. However, special substrate characteristics might require different powders in terms of color or other properties [1, pp. 136–137]. Other special forms of powdering include magnetic powders, which should cause less destruction by avoiding the brushing and wet powder, which can be applied on wet substrates in contrast to standard powdering techniques [1, p.137].

A chemical treatment for non-porous substrates is the cyanoacrylate fuming, also known as super glue fuming. This technique uses the effect of the polymerization of cyanoacrylate vapor at the fingerprint ridges. In particular, it reacts with eccrine and sebaceous components within the residue. The process is performed in special fuming chambers which provide a defined level of humidity and controlled heat sources for vaporizing the cyanoacrylate. It is the most commonly used technique for the latent mark development on non-porous substrates in laboratories [1, p. 138]. The result of this process is a hard white polymer on the ridges. Thus, after the fuming often an additional staining is applied to enhance the visibility of the developed marks.

The vacuum metal deposition technique is another method for visualizing latent marks on non-porous substrates [1, pp. 145–147]. The key aspect of this method is the effect that the finger mark residue hinders the deposition of metallic films. In this technique gold is evaporated under vacuum to form a thin layer of metal on the surface of an object. This layer is deposited across the surface and penetrates the residue which forms the mark. In a second step zinc is deposited in the same manner on the layer of gold. In contrast to the gold layer, this layer of zinc does not penetrate the fingerprint residue. Thus an increased contrast between the substrate and the mark is achieved. The result is usually a negative mark. An additional advantage of this technique is that it can be applied even after fuming the mark with cyanoacrylate.

On porous substrates the application of ninhydrin is one of the common detection techniques [1, pp. 114–124]. Ninhydrin reacts with amino acids, proteins and peptides within the residue resulting in a dark purple color. In the development process the substrate is often dipped into a solution of the reagent. Alternatively, the solution can be applied by spraying or brushing. Afterward, the samples are dried and stored at room temperature for several hours for developing the purple color caused by the chemical reaction. Besides ninhydrin, several analogs can be applied as well; diazafluorene (DFO), see e.g. [1, pp. 128–131] is one example for such an analog reagent.

An alternative to the ninhydrin treatment is the utilization of a physical developer [1, pp. 131–133]. This particular technique is sensitive to water insoluble components of the residue and hence applicable for wet surfaces as well. The technique is based on the photographic physical developer. Once the substrate is placed in the reagent, silver is slowly depositing on it. The residue increases the amount of the deposited silver, resulting in darker areas on the developed surface.

The multimetal deposition (MMD) technique is a two-step process [1, pp. 133–134]. In the first step gold is deposited on the fingerprint residue within a colloidal gold solution. In the second step a modified physical developer solution is used to amplify the visibility of the treated mark. This technique can be applied on porous and non-porous substrates.

After the development of the latent mark, it is usually acquired by taking photographs [24, pp. 3–38, 289–321]. Those photos are afterward developed or printed for the following investigation steps. Depending on the characteristics of the developed mark special illumination techniques can be applied for an additional enhanced contrast.

2.4 Contact-Less Latent Mark Acquisition Techniques

The contact-less acquisition of the latent marks has the same purpose as conventional acquisition techniques—detecting the mark and making it usable for a forensic analysis by latent print examiners (LPEs). The main difference is the selection of the means of processing the mark. In particular, contact-less techniques exploit physical/optical properties and the chemical composition of the residue which can be sensed without a direct contact with the mark. However, not every contact-less acquisition method can be considered non-destructive, see e.g. [24, pp. 294–295]. Especially the utilization of UV radiation is known for its potential impact on DNA traces within the mark. Several known contact-less approaches are selected and summarized in the remainder of this section.

Early experiments with detecting the inherent fingerprint luminescence with lasers date back to 1977 [25]. However, the high performance could only be reproduced for contaminated residues. Without such a contamination, less than 20% of the marks allowed for the detection of fingerprints by laser excited luminescent [26]. Similar to the luminescence the fluorescence of fingerprints can be investigated as well [24]. However, the quality of the results for untreated marks also depends on particular contaminations.

Other approaches exploit the diffuse reflection of light on the residue. Such approaches can be applied to recover latent marks from smooth, non-porous, glossy substrates such as glass, plastic or polished metals [1, p.112] or for recovering marks in dust [24]. Such examples include oblique illumination setups, dark field illumination, coaxial illumination and the usage of polarized light (see [24, 27]). Those illumination techniques are already applied in forensic practice to enhance the contrast of latent and developed marks.

Various ultraviolet imaging techniques are also used in today's police practice. The most commonly used UV imaging technique is the reflected UV imaging system (RUVIS), which usually employs shortwave UV radiation [24, pp. 289–299]. This approach utilizes specific UV absorption characteristics of the substrate and the residue as well as the diffuse reflection from the residue [1, pp. 112–113]. The results depend on the substrate, the angle of the light source and the type of the light source.

Another spectrum is used by the EVISCAN system [28]. The system employs a heat source emitting long wavelength infrared radiation and a high-resolution thermal vision camera to capture the diffuse reflection of IR radiation from the fingerprint in an oblique top measurement setup.

For glossy, curved substrates, [29] employ a gloss-meter and a rotary stage to acquire the finger marks. Such systems have the advantage of compensating the perspective distortion which would occur in normal 2D imaging.

The technique of optical coherence tomography can be used to detect latent marks covered by a layer of dust [30]. The sensor is able to produce 3D volume data of light scattering material.

The approach described in [31] utilizes the chemical composition of the residue in conjunction with Fourier transform infrared spectroscopy (FTIR). This technique allows for acquiring latent marks from various porous and non-porous substrates. However, the sensory has significant limitations regarding the size of the samples.

Within the scope of the German Federal Ministry of Education and Research funded research project "DigiDak" reflection based sensors are employed as well. The experiments use three different measurement principles: hyperspectral imaging in the UV to NIR range [32], chromatic confocal sensing [33] and confocal laser scanning microscopy [34]. The latter two techniques additionally allow for capturing height information (topography) from the latent marks or other types of traces. Due to the perpendicular illumination and measurement, those sensors primarily sense an intensity reduction on the areas covered with residue caused by the previously mentioned diffuse reflection of the latent mark.

As an outcome of this research project, a data set of computer generated finger marks is available upon request [35]. This particular data set consists of fingerprint patterns generated using SFinGe [36] which have been afterward printed on an overhead foil using artificial sweat and standard inkjet printers. Subsequently, each of the 24 samples has been contact-less acquired using a FRT MicroProf 200 surface measurement device equipped with a FRT CWL 600 sensor with a resolution of 500 and 1000 ppi.

A specific advantage of the non-destructive acquisition is the possibility to observe a mark over an interval of time by acquiring a series of scheduled images of it, called time series in [4]. This is a foundation for estimating the age of the mark by determining its speed of degradation [4]. Additionally, such degradation can be used to determine the persistence of finger marks on the surface of specific substrates.

Estimating the age of latent marks is an old challenge which has not been solved, yet. If it is possible to determine the age of a mark, the evidential value would increase significantly because it would be possible to prove that an individual has been at the crime scene at the time of the crime. In [4] time series of latent marks covering the first 24 h after the placement of the mark are the foundation for extracting 17 features. The feature space consists of binary pixel features from intensity and topography images as well as statistical features. The individual aging speed is determined by calculating ten consecutive feature values for each sample. The experimental setup consists of numerous donors and various influence factors. In the experiments two disjunct time classes are defined in order to determine whether the mark is younger or older than 5 h with different classifiers. Here, the classification accuracy for single features varies between 79.29% in the best case and 30.02% in the worst case. However, the performance can be slightly improved up to 83.10% if non-deterministic aging tendencies are excluded from the classification. For the combined feature space the classification accuracy varies between 65.08 and 79.79% depending on the amount of excluded time series.

Besides the age estimation of finger marks, the degradation of the residue of the mark can be used to locate traces within a temporal feature space. This particular location approach is motivated by the persistence of fibers at crime scenes. The foundation for the temporal feature space for latent marks are spectral texture features which are observed over a series of consecutive scans. For comparison, this feature space is also applied in the spatial domain. The general approach of using temporal features is similar to the age estimation. However, there are some differences within the processing pipeline. In contrast to the age estimation where a set of features is extracted from a series of samples, each sample is separated into blocks of 2 × 2 mm. Each block allows for determining the individual tendencies within the feature space in the region it is covering. In [37] the experiments are performed within low resolution scans (125 ppi) covering an area of 20 × 20 cm of the three (semi-)porous substrates copying paper, photographic paper and a textured catalog paper. Each substrate is prepared with 60 latent prints from six test subjects. The low acquisition resolution is necessary in order to achieve a reasonable acquisition time for each scan of 2.1 h for copying paper and 1.1 h for reflective photographic and catalog papers. The results for the three investigated substrates in [37] show an improved performance of the temporal feature space in comparison to the spatial feature space. The largest performance gain of 6.7% points is achieved when eight consecutive images are used to determine the temporal features. However, the results in [37] also indicate that a large number of consecutive scans might lead to a deteriorated performance as well.

2.5 Latent Mark Analysis Process

After the acquisition of the mark, usually a digital preprocessing is applied for an additional enhancement of the fingerprint pattern. Depending on the substrate, various artifacts might interfere with the pattern of the mark and the contrast within the image. Thus, emphasizing the fingerprint pattern can be quite challenging because the fingerprint is not necessarily the dominating pattern within the image as summarized in [33]. Hence the digital preprocessing of latent marks often significantly differs from the enhancement of exemplar prints as used in biometric systems. Moreover, it is not possible to ask the subject to acquire a sample with a better quality. These particular challenge are addressed in [38] for conventionally captured latent marks within the NIST Special Database 27 [39] or [40] for contact-less acquired marks using image processing and pattern recognition approaches.

The approach in [38] consists of a manual markup of the ROI, core and delta points, the block-based computation of multiple dominant orientations utilizing the short-time Fourier transform, the orientation field estimation using R-RANSAC and subsequently the enhancement by employing Gabor filters. The hypothesis creation and evaluation for determining the orientation fields using R-RANSAC is necessary to detect a plausible ridge flow. Otherwise parts of the background orientations might be mixed with the fingerprint orientations which possibly alter minutiae points. The last step of utilizing Gabor filters is known from the processing of exemplar prints in biometric systems as well. Here, on the foundation of the local ridge frequency and orientation the fingerprint pattern can be emphasized.

The approach in [40] utilizes the whole amount of available data from the contact-less sensory, namely the intensity and topography image. In contrast to [38] no human interaction is necessary to process the image of the mark during its processing. The first step of this approach is the preprocessing of each input image using various Sobel operators, unsharp masking and various Gabor filters. Each preprocessed image is afterwards processed separately. The feature extraction for the pattern recognition based decision whether a block contains fingerprint residue or not is performed in blocks of 50×50 μm. The feature space consists of statistical, structural and fingerprint semantics features. Afterward, each block is classified using pre-trained models. Subsequently, a fingerprint image can be reconstructed based on the classifiers decisions. The primary challenge of this approach is the training of the classifiers. This step is time-consuming and usually requires human interaction in order to get a ground-truth for the supervised learning. The evaluation is performed for eight different substrates ranging from the rather cooperative white furniture surface to the very challenging blued metal and golden oak veneer. In the best case, a classification accuracy of 95.1% is achieved. On golden oak at least an accuracy of 81.1% is achieved. However, an automated biometric feature extraction and matching is only successful for fingerprints from three of the eight substrates.

Another challenge for the preprocessing is the handling of overlapping marks. Such marks frequently appear on locations which are often touched. Such places can be door handles, elevator buttons or touch screens. In current police practice such traces are usually discarded if the non-overlapped region of the mark does not contain a sufficient amount of minutiae points.

One of the first approaches addressing this challenge to separate two overlapping patterns is published in [2]. This approach is designed for conventionally captured marks. During the first step it is necessary to mark the region mask manually. Here, the two non-overlapped and the overlapped regions are defined by the user. Afterward, the initial orientation field is determined which contains two orientation labels within the overlapped region. The separation of the overlapped orientation field is performed using a relaxation labeling algorithm resulting in two component fingerprints which need to be constructed using compatibility coefficients based on the local neighborhood of each block or object. After this step, the separated orientation fields are merged with the orientation fields of the non-overlapped regions.

An extended separation approach for conventionally and contact-less acquired marks is proposed in [3]. Here, the context-based computation and optimization of parameters are introduced, e.g. for accounting for different acquisition resolutions. The biometric evaluation of the separation results show an equal error rate of 5.7% for contact-less acquired marks, and 17.9% for conventionally captured marks. These results show that the separation benefits from the increased acquisition resolution of 2540 ppi of the contact-less acquired latent marks.

For the analysis of the latent marks, usually the ACE-V process (see [41]) or variations of it, is applied. ACE-V is an abbreviation for the four processing stages: analysis, comparison, evaluation and verification.

During the first step, the analysis, the acquired latent mark is investigated regarding the overall quality and the clarity and number of usable features. Several influence factors, such as the substrate, the development medium, assumed deposition pressure or distortions, are taken into account in this step. If the latent print examiner comes to the conclusion that the quality is too low, e.g., due to a lack of sufficient features, the mark is discarded as insufficient without performing the remaining steps of the ACE-V process. Otherwise it is compared to a reference print in the following step.

The comparison step (2nd step) involves a side-by-side comparison between two fingerprint patterns—usually represented by the latent mark from a crime scene and a reference print with a known origin connected with an identity. During the first comparison step, the level 1 pattern is compared. The comparison can be aborted if those patterns do not match; if the patterns are identical or not visible in one of the samples, the comparison is continued by creating relationships between level 2 features. However, due to potential distortions and low-quality areas this is usually no physical measurement with a fixed scale and thus hard to automate. The features are usually matched by following ridge paths or by counting ridges between two feature points. The matching itself is a subjective process which requires extensive training. Especially for poor quality marks the tolerance for variations is increased, which usually requires an increased number of features in order to decide about the result of the comparison in the next step.

The third step for the latent print examination is the evaluation. This step contains the formulation of the final conclusion based on the analysis and comparison steps of the samples. The examiner has to decide whether both patterns originate from the same source. This also requires the explanation of differences and variations found during the comparison. If the level 1, 2 and 3 features are sufficiently similar between the two prints the conclusion is called individualization. Likewise, if a number of different features are found and not explainable, e.g., by distortions, the conclusion is called exclusion which means that the patterns originate from different fingers. The result is marked as inconclusive if the examiner is unable to make a decision beyond reasonable doubt, e.g., due to a lack of matching and non-matching features.

The last (fourth) step of the ACE-V process is the verification. This step is performed because the comparison of the two fingerprint patterns is a subjective process. The verification consists of an independent analysis, a comparison and an evaluation of the samples by a second examiner. It is intended to increase the reliability of the final conclusion by reducing the subjectivity of the decision. This ideally means that the second investigator is unaware of the initial investigation results. If both examiners warrant the same conclusion, the examination of the latent mark is finished. Otherwise, a third examiner might repeat the investigation or the outcomes can be discussed and reevaluated by the two examiners in order to find an agreement.

The requirements for the decision-making are different in various countries. Currently two standards exist [42]: the numerical standard and the non-numerical standard.

The numerical standard defines a minimum number of matching level 2 feature points in order to draw the conclusion of identification. However, the threshold regarding the number of necessary features varies between 7 and 17 [42, p. 47]. This fixed threshold does not account for the rarity of particular feature points. Thus, the conclusion can be drawn from a specific number of rather common feature points or from rarer features as well. In order to account for this discrepancy in the evidential value of the features, some countries have switched to non-numerical standards [43]. This results in dynamic thresholds based on, e.g., the specificity of the features considering the rarity of feature points and the relationship to other points. In other words: a smaller number of matching rare features can suffice for drawing the conclusion of identification whereas a large number of matching common features might result in an inconclusive outcome. Thus, the non-numerical standard provides an increased flexibility in the decision making. However, on the other hand this results in an increased responsibility for the examiner and the requirement to provide sufficient statistical data and sophisticated knowledge of the state of the art to back the decision.

2.6 Legal Challenges of Applying New Techniques in the Latent Mark Processing

Each new procedure in forensics needs to be evaluated regarding their suitability and scientific foundation. In the US, a so-called Daubert challenge (see [44]) is known which can be used to assess the suitability of a scientific method prior to the admission of the evidence in court. In such a Daubert challenge at the Supreme Court, the judge has a role of a gatekeeper to screen scientific evidence in order to ensure that only relevant and reliable sources are admitted. In the original trial of Daubert v. Merrell Dow Pharmaceuticals in 1993 a list of five factors was provided, which a judge might consider during the assessment of the scientific validity of the theory or method [44]:

- *Whether it [the method] can be (and has been) tested,*
- *Whether it has been subjected to peer review and publication,*
- *The known or potential rate of error [of the method],*
- *The existence and maintenance of standards controlling the technique's operation,*
- *Whether it is generally accepted in the scientific community.*

This list has been extended after the initial Daubert decision by additional factors as summarized in [44, p. 38]. For new acquisition techniques this would require an extensive testing and the definition of particular standards. This would also require a comparison with existing techniques to show the validity of the results. Here, the contact-less acquisition techniques have the advantage that they would not interfere with any other conventional detection technique. Thus, it is possible to acquire the mark by non-destructive means in the first place and to verify the results using accepted standard procedures afterward.

However, in the context of the latent mark examination in general a critical review of court rulings is given in [45]. In the essence of [45] the fingerprint evidence merits its acceptance in court due to its long usage of over a century even if it would hardly withstand a careful evaluation of the Daubert factors. In [46] the rate of error is investigated in more detail. The author describes multiple cases of erroneous identifications indicating a non-zero error rate. However, he also states that the available data is inadequate to calculate a meaningful error rate. A solution to account for the non-zero error rate is the usage of known likelihood ratios (LR): instead of presenting the result of a binary decision, a quotient between the probabilities of two opposing hypotheses is given.

In the context of fingerprints [10], the two hypotheses are that the patterns originate from the same finger or from different fingers. Especially the variability of the pattern due to skin elasticity needs to be taken into account for determining the probabilities. In such an LR-based approach, the outcome of exclusion would relate to an LR of zero, whereas identification relates to an LR of infinity (due to the assumed error rate of zero). In practice the likelihood ratio is somewhere between those two extremes due to the variability of the patterns.

Although the first experiments in [10] look promising, they suffer from a challenge in a real-world application: it is almost impossible to calculate the probability for the two patterns originating from different fingers as the denominator for determining the LR since it would require knowing the patterns and properties of all fingers in the world. Thus, it is only possible to estimate this probability. Nevertheless, the application of LRs helps to express uncertainties in the decision process, see e.g. [47].

2.7 Summary

This chapter summarizes a selection of the state of the art of the latent mark acquisition and analysis. Even though the comparison of fingerprints has a long tradition in forensic investigations, several crucial questions remain unanswered to date. From a technical point of view, a broad variety of sensors allow for acquiring latent marks without the need for altering the trace composition by adding additional reagents. On the other hand, such techniques require an extensive testing in line with best practices of the police forces before they can replace the conventional techniques. Nevertheless, non-destructive sensors allow for new investigation techniques such as the age estimation or the observation of the fingerprint persistency.

The comparison of the fingerprint patterns bears several challenges as well. Especially the elasticity of the skin is a cause for uncertainty in the decision-making process. Here, it is necessary to establish a statistical foundation to determine likelihood ratios based on a common standard to be able to express and consider potential uncertainties while retaining a comparability of the resulting values.

With respect to the legal requirements there is currently no common ground. Some countries employ the numerical standard with thresholds requiring between 7 and 17 matching features [42, p. 47]. Others use non-numeric standards which account for the specificity of particular feature points.

References

1. Champod C, Lennard C, Margot P, Stoilovic M (2004) Fingerprints and other ridge skin impressions. CRC Press
2. Chen F, Feng J, Jain AK, Zhou J, Zhang J (2011) Separating overlapped fingerprints. IEEE Trans Inf Forensics Secur 6(2):346–359
3. Qian K, Schott M, Zheng W, Dittmann J (2014) A context-based approach of separating contactless captured high-resolution overlapped fingerprints. IET Biom 3(2):101–112
4. Merkel R, Gruhn S, Dittmann J, Vielhauer C, Bräutigam A (2012) On non-invasive 2D and 3D chromatic white light image sensors for age determination of latent fingerprints. Forensic Sci Int 222(1–3):52–70

5. Harper W (1937) Fingerprint forgery—transferred latent fingerprints. J Criminol 28(4): 573–580
6. Wertheim PA (1994) Latent fingerprint fabrication, website request 12/02/2016, see also in Wertheim, Pat A., Detection of Forged and Fabricated Fingerprints. J Forensic Ident, 44(6), pp 652–681. http://www.iowaiai.org/latent-fingerprint-fabrication/
7. Champod C, Espinoza M (2014) Forgeries of fingerprints in forensic science, In: Marcel S, Nixon MS, Li SZ (eds) Handbook of biometric anti-spoofing, ser. advances in computer vision and pattern recognition. Springer, London, pp 13–34
8. Hildebrandt M, Dittmann J (2015) StirTraceV2.0: enhanced benchmarking and tuning of printed fingerprint detection. IEEE Trans Inf Forensics Secur 10(4):833–848
9. Modi SK, Elliott SJ, Whetsone J, Kim H (2007) Impact of age groups on fingerprint recognition performance. In: IEEE workshop on automatic identification advanced technologies, pp 19–23
10. Neumann C, Champod C, Puch-Solis R, Egli N, Anthonioz A, Bromage-Griffiths A (2007) Computation of likelihood ratios in fingerprint identification for configurations of any number of minutiae. J Forensic Sci 52(1):54–64
11. Jain AK, Flynn P, Ross A (2008) Handbook of biometrics. Springer, US
12. Ross A, Jain AK (2004) Biometric sensor interoperability: a case study in fingerprints. In: International workshop on biometric authentication: ECCV 2004, pp 134–145
13. Mayer JCA (1788) Anatomische Kupfertafeln: nebst dazu gehörigen Erklärungen (Band 4): Eilf Kupfertafeln von den Sinnwerkzeugen und den Brüsten. Berlin, Leipzig, Universitätsbibliothek Heidelberg. http://digi.ub.uni-heidelberg.de/diglit/mayer1788bd4/0006
14. Purkinje JE (1823) Commentatio de examine physiologico organi visus et systematis cutanei: quam pro loco in gratioso medicorum ordine rite obtinendo die XXII. decembris MDCCCXXIII, H.X.L.C. Vratislaviae: Typus Universitatis. https://archive.org/details/68020950R.nlm.nih.gov
15. Herschel W J (1916) The origin of finger-printing. Oxford University Press. http://galton.org/fingerprints/books/herschel/herschel-1916-origins-1up.pdf
16. Faulds H (1880) On the skin-furrows of the hand. Nature (Oct. 28 1880), p. 605
17. Galton F (1892) Finger prints. Macmillan and Co
18. Henry ER (1900) Classification and uses of finger prints. George Routledge and Sons https://archive.org/details/ClassificationAndUsesOfFingerPrints
19. Rudin N, Inman K (2016) The forensic science timeline. http://www.forensicdna.com/timeline.html, Accessed 02 Dec 2016
20. Kingston CR, Kirk PL (1965) Historical development and evaluation of the '12 point rule' in fingerprint identification. Int Crim Police Rev
21. Ashbaugh DR (1999) Ridgeology: modern evaluative friction ridge identification. Royal Canadian Mounted Police, Forensic Identification Support Section
22. Inman K, Rudin N (2000) Principles and practice of criminalistics: the profession of forensic science (Protocols in forensic science). CRC Press
23. Zhao Q, Jain AK (2010) On the utility of extended fingerprint features: a study on pores. In: Computer vision and pattern recognition workshops (CVPRW), pp 9–16
24. Bleay SM, Sears VG, Bandey HL, Gibson AP, Bowman VJ, Downham R, Fitzgerald L, Ciuksza T, Ramadani J, Selway C (2012) Fingerprint source book. Home Office CAST, United Kingdom
25. Dalrymple BE, Duff JM, Menzel ER (1977) Inherent fingerprint luminescence—detection by laser. J Forensic Sci 22:106–115
26. Salares VR, Eves CR, Carey PR (1979) On the detection of fingerprints by laser excited luminescence. Forensic Sci Int 14:229–237
27. Lin S-S, Yemelyanov KM, Pugh EN Jr, Engheta N (2006) Polarization-based and specular-reflection-based noncontact latent fingerprint imaging and lifting. J Opt Soc Am A 23(9):2137–2153
28. German eForensics GmbH, EVISCAN contactless evidence detection. https://www.eviscan.com/files/71/eviscan-brochure-lowres.pdf, Accessed 29 Dec 2015

29. Kuivalainen K, Peiponen K-E, Myller K (2009) Application of a diffractive element-based sensor for detection of latent fingerprints from a curved smooth surface. Meas Sci Technol 20 (7):077002
30. Dubey SK, Mehta DS, Anand A, Shakher C (2008) Simultaneous topography and tomography of latent fingerprints using full-field swept-source optical coherence tomography. J Opt A: Pure Appl Opt, 10(1), 015 307–015 315
31. Crane NJ, Bartick EG, Perlman RS, Huffman S (2007) Infrared spectroscopic imaging for noninvasive detection of latent fingerprints. J Forensic Sci 52(1):48–53
32. Makrushin A, Scheidat T, Vielhauer C (2015) Capturing latent fingerprints from metallic painted surfaces using UV-VIS spectroscope. In: Proceedings of SPIE 9409: media watermarking, security, and forensics 2015
33. Hildebrandt M, Merkel R, Leich M, Kiltz S, Dittmann J, Vielhauer C (2011) Benchmarking contact-less surface measurement devices for fingerprint acquisition in forensic investigations: results for a differential scan approach with a chromatic white light sensor. In: Proceedings of DSP'11, pp 1–6
34. Kirst S, Vielhauer C (2015) Detection of latent fingerprints using high-resolution 3D confocal microscopy in non-planar acquisition scenarios. In: Proceedings of SPIE 9409: media watermarking, security, and forensics 2015
35. Hildebrandt M, Sturm J, Dittmann J, Vielhauer C (2013) Creation of a public corpus of contact-less acquired latent fingerprints without privacy implications. Commun Multimedia Secur, LNCS 8099:204–206
36. Cappelli R (2015) Fingerprint sample synthesis. In: Li SZ Jain AK (eds) Encyclopedia of biometrics, 2nd edn. Springer
37. Merkel R, Dittmann J, Hildebrandt M (2014) Latent fingerprint persistence: a new temporal feature space for forensic trace evidence analysis. In: IEEE international conference on image processing (ICIP), Paris pp. 4952–4956. doi: 10.1109/ICIP.2014.7026003
38. Yoon S, Feng J, Jain AK (2011) Latent fingerprint enhancement via robust orientation field estimation. In: 2011 international joint conference on biometrics (IJCB), pp 1–8
39. National Institute of Standards and Technology NIST special database 27 [Online]. https://www.nist.gov/srd/nist-special-database-27
40. Hildebrandt M, Kiltz S, Dittmann J, Vielhauer C (2014) An enhanced feature set for pattern recognition based contrast enhancement of contact-less captured latent fingerprints in digitized crime scene forensics. In: Proceedings of SPIE 9028: media watermarking, security, and forensics 2014
41. Holder EH, Robinson LO, Laub JH (eds.) (2011) The fingerprint sourcebook, US Department of Justice, Office of Justice Programs, National Institute of Justice, NCJ 225320
42. Polski J, Smith R, Garrett R, et al (2011) The report of the international association for identification, standardization II committee. Document No. 233980. https://www.ncjrs.gov/pdffiles1/nij/grants/233980.pdf, Accessed 30 Dec 2015
43. BBC News (2006) Court fingerprint system scrapped. http://news.bbc.co.uk/2/hi/uk_news/scotland/5310246.stm, Accessed 30 Dec 2015
44. Dixon L, Gill B (2001) Changes in the standards for admitting expert evidence in federal civil cases since the daubert decision. rand institute for civil justice
45. Benedict N (2004) fingerprints and the daubert standard for admission of scientific evidence: why fingerprints fail and a proposed remedy. Ariz Law Rev 46(3):519–549
46. Cole SA (2005) More than zero: accounting for error in latent fingerprint identification. J Crim Law Criminol 95(3):985–1078
47. Martire KA, Kemp RI, Sayle M, Newell BR (2014) On the interpretation of likelihood ratios in forensic science evidence: presentation formats and the weak evidence effect. In: Forensic science international, vol 240, pp 61–68

Chapter 3
Automated Fingerprint Identification Systems: From Fingerprints to Fingermarks

Davide Maltoni, Raffaele Cappelli and Didier Meuwly

Abstract The aim of this chapter is to present the automated fingerprint recognition technology and its use for forensic applications. After a brief historical review, we provide an introduction to modern Automated Fingerprint Identification Systems (AFIS) by discussing their functionalities and accuracy. The topic then becomes more technical and goes through some of the recently introduced approaches for fingerprint recognition (both for fingerprint and fingermarks). Forensic applications exploiting the recognition of fingerprints (identity verification and identification) and fingermarks (forensic intelligence, investigation and evaluation) are then described. Finally, a discussion about the current topics and foreseeable challenges in terms of technology and application concludes the chapter.

3.1 Introduction

3.1.1 History

In the early twentieth century, fingerprint recognition was formally accepted as a valid personal identification method and became a standard routine in forensic science [1]. Fingerprint identification agencies were set up worldwide and criminal fingerprint databases were established [1]. Various fingerprint recognition techniques, including fingermark[1] processing, fingerprint classification, and fingerprint

[1]The finger dermatoglyphics and their standard rolled or flat inked or scanned impressions are named *fingerprints*, whereas the recovered or lifted traces are named *fingermarks* (latent fingerprints is a popular but imprecise synonym for fingermarks) [2].

D. Maltoni (✉) · R. Cappelli
Ingegneria e Scienze Informatiche, Università di Bologna, Via Sacchi 3, 47521, Cesena, Forlì-Cesena, Italy
e-mail: maltoni@csr.unibo.it

D. Meuwly
Services, Cybersecurity and Safety, Netherlands Forensic Institute, University of Twente, Drienerlolaan 5, 7522, NB Enschede, The Netherlands

M. Tistarelli and C. Champod (eds.), *Handbook of Biometrics for Forensic Science*, Advances in Computer Vision and Pattern Recognition,
DOI 10.1007/978-3-319-50673-9_3

comparison were developed. For example, in the US, the FBI fingerprint identification division was set up in 1924 with a database of 810,000 fingerprint cards (see [3, 4]).

With the rapid expansion of fingerprint recognition in forensic science, operational fingerprint databases became so huge that manual fingerprint identification turned to be infeasible. For example, the total number of fingerprint cards (each card contains one impression for each of the 10 fingers of a person) in the FBI fingerprint database now stands well over 200 million from its original number of 810,000 and is growing continuously. With thousands of requests being received daily, even a team of more than 1300 fingerprint experts were not able to provide timely responses to these requests [1]. Starting in the early 1960s, the FBI, Home Office in the UK, Paris Police Department in France, and the National Police Agency of Japan, began to invest a large amount of effort in developing automatic fingerprint identification systems [1]. In 1963, FBI Special Agent Carl Voelker asked the assistance of NIST engineers Raymond Moore and Joe Wegstein to study the first automated solution for fingerprint identification. Moore and Wegstein analyzed the manual methods used by human fingerprint experts, mainly based on comparing minutiae (i.e. ridge endings and ridge bifurcations) on fingerprint ridges [5]. If the minutiae from two fingerprints were determined to be topologically equivalent, the two fingerprints were declared to be from the same finger of the same person. Based on the above observations, three major problems in designing AFISs were identified: digital fingerprint acquisition, minutiae extraction, and minutiae comparison. During 15 years of work on this topic, Wegstein developed and improved some minutiae comparison algorithms [6–13], including the well-known M82 comparison algorithm [13]. In the same period, some companies and organizations started developing AFIS components and prototypes, responding to requests issued by government agencies. By the early 1990s, four major vendors leaded the AFIS market: Printrak and Cogent (US), Morpho (France), and NEC (Japan). AFIS rapidly evolved from initial vendor-specific prototypes to efficient and interoperable systems able to process millions identification requests per second. Today almost every law enforcement agency in the developed and most emerging countries uses an AFIS. Large-scale civil projects (such as India UIDAI) also make use of these technologies. These systems have greatly improved the operational productivity of law enforcement agencies and reduced the cost of hiring and training human fingerprint experts.

3.1.2 AFIS Functionalities

The basic functions of a modern AFIS are:

- *Single/multiprint identification*—identifying a single fingerprint (or a set of fingerprints) from an individual to determine where (s)he has an existing record in the system. Depending on the application and the required identification

accuracy, a variable number of fingerprints of the same individual can be used (typically 1, 2, 4, 8 or 10).
- *Fingermark search*—attempting to link fingermarks to other fingermarks or to single/multiprint cards.

In both cases the result provided by the system is a candidate list of a given length, sorted according to a comparison score. The relationship between a score and the probability of correct identification is still debated, as discussed in Sect. 3.3. Possible enhanced functions provided by recent AFIS include:

- *Palmprint/mark search*—adding palmprint records to the database to allow search of pamprints/marks.
- *Multimodal identification systems*—combining the recognition of several biometric modalities (fingerprint, palmprint, iris, and face).

In forensic science these AFIS functionalities are exploited inside several processes [2]:

- **Identity verification**, that is a *decision* about the identity of a person based on the comparison of her/his fingerprints;
- **Forensic intelligence**, that is an *association* of criminal cases through fingermarks and palmmarks;
- **Forensic investigation,** that is a *selection* of candidates on the basis of the comparison of finger- and palmmarks recovered on a crime scene with a database of finger- and palmprints;
- **Forensic evaluation,** that is a *description* of the strength of evidence resulting from the study, using a comparative approach of the similarity and the distinctiveness of a fingermark recovered on a crime scene and a fingerprint of a candidate selected during the forensic investigation process. It seeks individualization but remains probabilistic and inductive in essence [14].

3.1.3 Fingerprint Identification Accuracy

Identification accuracy in AFIS open-set scenario[2] is typically denoted by the value of FNIR when the system is tuned to operate at a given FPIR. Let t be a security threshold, then:

- False negative identification rate (FNIR) is the fraction of the mated searches where the enrolled mate is outside the candidate list, or is inside the list but its score is less than t;

[2]In open-set scenarios, some of the searched users have not a record in the database (*non-mated* search), while in closed-set scenarios it is assumed to search only users with at least one record in the database (*mated search*).

- The false positive identification rate (FPIR) is the fraction of the non-mated searches where one or more enrolled identities are returned in the candidate list with score higher than *t*.

Another common way to characterize AFIS accuracy is Rank-*n* metrics, denoting the percentage of mated searches where the correct identity is returned in the first *n* positions of the candidate list.

For more details refer to Sect. 6.1 of [15].

Several independent evaluation campaigns have been organized on fingerprint recognition since the year 2000 (see Sect. 4.7.2 of [16]). Referring to identification on large databases, one of the most comprehensive tests is FPVTE 2012 [15]. State-of-the-art algorithms from leading AFIS vendors have been submitted and evaluated on several tasks. The most accurate fingerprint identification algorithms achieved false negative identification rates (FNIR, or "miss rates") of:

- 1.9% for single index fingers,
- 0.27% for two index fingers,
- 0.45% for four-finger identification flats (IDFlats),
- 0.15% for eight-finger IDFlats,
- 0.05% for ten-finger IDFlats,
- 0.1% for ten-finger rolled-to-rolled,
- 0.13% for ten-finger plain-to-plain,
- 0.11% for ten-finger plain-to-rolled.

These numbers are reported at a false positive identification rate (FPIR) of 0.1%. 30,000 search subjects were used for these results (10,000 mates and 20,000 nonmates). The number of enrolled subjects used for single index fingers was 100,000,1.6 million for two index fingers, 3 million for IDFlats, and 5 million for ten-finger plains and rolled. A larger test with a search set of 50,000 mates and 300,000 nonmates has been scheduled so that accuracy at a smaller FPIR can be reported.

3.2 Automated Fingerprint/Mark Technology

3.2.1 Fingerprints

The block diagram of a typical fingerprint-based recognition system is depicted in Fig. 3.1.

Historically, in law enforcement applications, the acquisition of fingerprint images was performed by using the so-called "ink-technique": the subject's fingers were covered with black ink and pressed or rolled on a paper card; the card was then scanned by using a general-purpose scanner, producing a digital image. This kind of acquisition process is referred to as off-line fingerprint acquisition. Nowadays, most AFIS accept live-scan digital images acquired by directly sensing

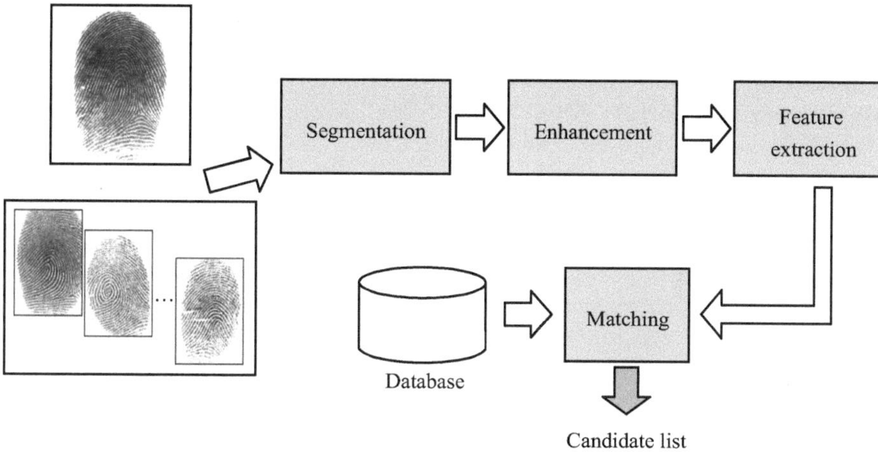

Fig. 3.1 Block diagram of a fingerprint-based recognition system, where the input can be a single fingerprint or a set of fingerprints

the finger surface with an electronic fingerprint scanner. Appropriate image quality requirements for AFIS fingerprint scanners were defined by the FBI in Appendix F of the Electronic Fingerprint Transmission Specification (EFTS) [17]. Depending on the operating modality (single or multiprint identification), the input consists of one or more input raw images. Single fingerprints can be acquired as *plain* (or *flat*) representations or in *rolled* representation, which is characterized by an unwrapped nail-to-nail pattern.

In the following, the main processing steps applied to each raw image are summarized. The raw image is first passed to an image enhancement module, whose goal is to improve the clarity of the ridge pattern, especially in noisy regions, to simplify the subsequent feature extraction. Special digital filtering techniques, known as contextual filtering [16], are usually adopted at this stage. The feature extraction module further processes the enhanced image and extracts a set of features from it. This feature set often includes minutiae but, depending on the comparison algorithm, other features (e.g. local orientation, local frequency, singularities, ridge shapes, ridge counts, parts of the enhanced image, sweat pores, etc.) can be extracted too. It has been recently proved that using extended features [18, 19] in combination with minutiae can lead to better accuracy [20, 21].

Finally, the matching module compares the extracted features against all records in the database. Comparing two fingerprints typically requires finding the spatial correspondence of a minimum number of minutiae; this is not a simple task because of the large variations (e.g. displacement, rotation, skin condition, distortion, noise, etc.) that can characterize two fingerprints acquired from the same finger at different times. Earlier comparison algorithms try to find a suitable alignment by maximizing minutiae pairing at global level (i.e. throughout the whole fingerprint pattern). Nowadays the most effective algorithms first compare local arrangements of minutiae and then consolidate them at global level [16]. This improves efficiency and better tolerates skin distortion.

A recently proposed effective algorithm is based on the Minutia Cylinder-Code (MCC) representation [22]. MCC builds a local descriptor for each minutia $m_i = (x_i, y_i, \theta_i)$, where (x_i, y_i) is the minutia location and θ_i is the minutia direction (in the range $[0, 2\pi[$). The descriptor encodes spatial and directional relationships between the minutia and its neighbourhood of radius R, and can be conveniently represented as a cylinder, whose base and height are related to the spatial and directional information, respectively (see Fig. 3.2a, b). The cylinder is divided into N_D sections: each section corresponds to a directional difference in the range $[-\pi, \pi[$; sections are discretized into cells (N_S is the number of cells along the section diameter). During the cylinder creation, a numerical value is calculated for each cell: it represents the likelihood of finding minutiae that are close to the cell and whose directional difference with respect to m_i is similar to a given value. Figure 3.2c, d shows the cylinder associated to a minutia with six minutiae in its neighbourhood. Once a cylinder is built from a minutia m_i, it can be simply treated as a single feature vector, obtained by linearizing the cell values. With a negligible loss of accuracy (see [23, 24]), each element of the feature vector can be stored as a bit (Fig. 3.2e): in the following, $\mathbf{v}_i \in \{0, 1\}^n$ denotes an MCC bit-vector obtained from minutia m_i, and $T = \{c_i\}$, denotes an *MCC template* obtained from a fingerprint, where each $c_i = (\mathbf{v}_i, x_i, y_i, \theta_i)$ is a tuple containing a bit-vector and its associated minutia information. Note that, although strictly speaking the term "cylinder" corresponds to $\mathbf{v}_i$ [22], in the following, for simplicity, it denotes the whole tuple c_i.

Each bit-vector $\mathbf{v}_i$ is a fixed-length local descriptor:

- invariant for translation and rotation, since (i) it only encodes distances and directional differences between minutiae, and (ii) its base is rotated according to the corresponding minutia angle;
- robust against skin distortion (which is small at a local level) and against small feature extraction errors, thanks to the smoothed nature of the functions defining the contribution of each minutia.

As described in [22], a simple but effective similarity measure between two cylinders $c_i = (\mathbf{v}_i, x_i, y_i, \theta_i)$ and $c_j = (\mathbf{v}_j, x_j, y_j, \theta_j)$ is:

$$s_L(c_i, c_j) = \begin{cases} 1 - \frac{\|\mathbf{v}_i \oplus \mathbf{v}_j\|}{\|\mathbf{v}_i\| + \|\mathbf{v}_j\|} & \text{if } d_\phi(\theta_i, \theta_j) \leq \delta_\theta \\ 0 & \text{otherwise} \end{cases}. \quad (1)$$

where

$\oplus$ Denotes the bitwise XOR operator;

$\|\cdot\|$ Denotes the Euclidean norm;

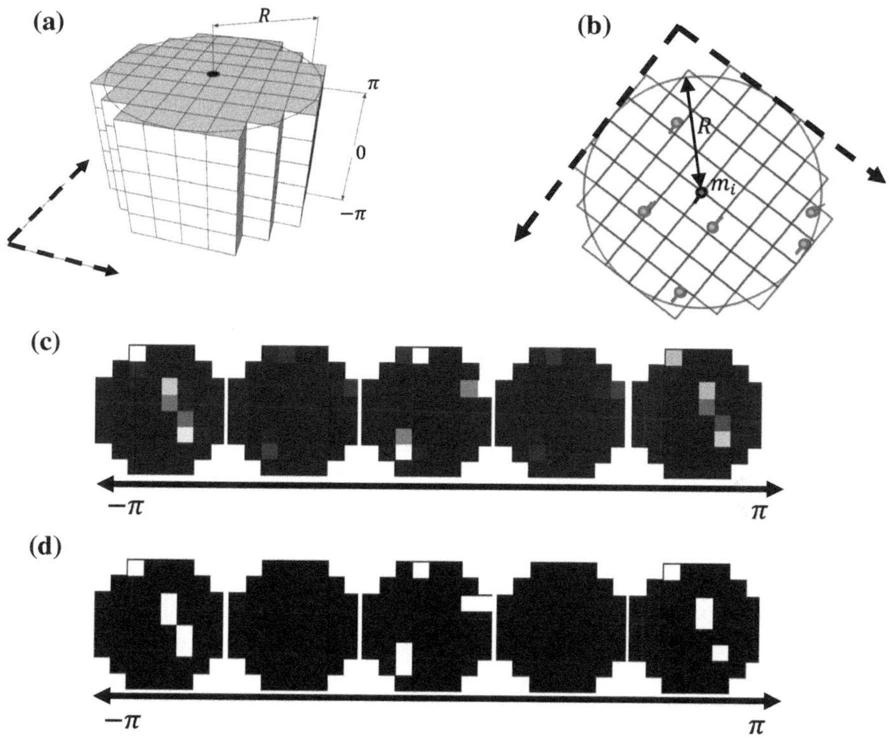

Fig. 3.2 **a** a graphical representation of the local descriptor associated to a minutia in the MCC representation, with $N_S = 8$ and $N_D = 5$; **b** minutiae involved in a cylinder; **c** cell values in the N_D sections (*lighter areas* represent higher values) of the *cylinder* built over the minutiae in (**b**); **d** binarized cell values stored as bits. Note that cylinder sections in (**c**) and (**d**) are rotated according to the direction of minutia m_i

$d_\phi(\theta_i, \theta_j)$ is the difference between the two angles;
δ_θ is a parameter controlling the maximum rotation allowed between two fingerprints

Note that (1) is a *local* similarity measure between two cylinders: in order to compare two fingerprint templates T_A and T_B, a single value (*global score*), denoting the overall fingerprint similarity, has to be obtained from the pairwise (local) cylinder similarities. Various global similarity measures have been proposed for MCC [22, 23, 25]; the simplest and most efficient one is the *Local Similarity Sort* (LSS), which is calculated as the average of the top local similarity scores between cylinders of the two templates. A more accurate, but less efficient, similarity measure is the *Local Similarity Sort with Distortion-Tolerant Relaxation* (LSS-DTR) [25]. LSS-DTR adds a consolidation step to LSS, in order to obtain a score that reflects to what extent the local similarities hold at global level. LSS-DTR is based on similarity measures between candidate pairs of corresponding minutiae

Table 3.1 Published parallel fingerprint identification methods on various hardware architecture: the throughput is expressed in million fingerprint comparisons per second, each speedup is measured with respect to a corresponding baseline sequential CPU implementation

Method	Hardware	Throughput	Speedup
Lindoso et al. [69]	FPGA Xilinx Virtex-4 LX	0.007	24
Jiang and Crookes [70]	FPGA Xilinx Virtex-E	1.220	47
Peralta et al. [71]	Cluster of 12 PC	0.813	181
Gutierrez et al. [72]	One Tesla M2090 GPU	0.050	31
	Two Tesla M2090 GPUs	0.098	61
Cappelli et al. [26]	One Tesla C2075 GPU	9.305	514
	Four Tesla C2075 GPUs	35.221	1 946

and uses spatial and directional features that are invariant for rotation/translation and tolerate skin distortion.

Owing to its bitwise fixed-length features and simple similarity metrics, MCC allows very fast fingerprint identification methods to be developed. In [26], an extremely fast MCC-based algorithm for graphic processing unit (GPU) is introduced. Thanks to a careful design of the algorithm, ad hoc data structures and lookup tables, special sorting methods and other optimizations, this algorithm is able to compare more than nine million fingerprint per second on a single GPU. Table 3.1 reports results published in the scientific literature for recent parallel fingerprint identification algorithms on various hardware architectures; it is well evident that the MCC-based algorithm described in [26] overcomes all the other approaches, both in terms of absolute performance and of relative speedup. In particular, on a single PC with four GPUs, it achieved a throughput of more than 35 million fingerprint comparisons per second; with such a throughput, less than 0.3 s are required to perform ten queries on a database with one million fingerprints, thus enabling real-time fingerprint identification on large databases with low-cost hardware.

3.2.2 *Fingermarks*

Fingermarks are partial impressions of the finger left on the surface of objects when they are touched. When invisible (latent), they are detected with optical methods and/or developed chemical/physical techniques before to be either captured photographically or lifted from objects. They are of critical value in forensic applications because they are usually encountered at crime scenes and serve as crucial evidence in a court of law.

However, compared to fingerprint comparison, fingermark comparison accuracy is significantly lower due to complex background noise, poor ridge quality and small area. As an example, in recent NIST evaluations, while the best-performing fingerprint algorithms achieved a rank-1 identification rate of about 99% on a background database of 100,000 fingerprints [15], the best-performing commercial fingermark comparison algorithm achieved a rank-1 identification rate of 67.2% when searching 1,066 fingermarks against a background database of 100,000 exemplar prints, without using manually annotated features [19].

In the current generation of AFIS, to make fingermark identification more reliable, manual markup of various features (e.g. region of interest, singular points and minutiae) is typically necessary. To reduce this markup cost and to improve the consistency, fully automatic ("lights-out") and highly accurate fingermark comparison algorithms are needed: "lights-out" capability for fingermark identification is one the major objectives of FBI's Next Generation Identification (NGI) program. In the last five years, research has been very active in fingermark processing and relevant steps have been done toward the practical implementation of systems operating in lights-out mode. In the Netherlands, for example, more than 60% of the pairing of fingermarks and reference fingerprints is obtained using automatic encoding only [2].

Referring to the general schema of Fig. 3.1, what makes fingermark identification different from traditional fingerprint identification is not the comparison step but the segmentation, enhancement and feature extraction stages. In fact, in principle, the comparison algorithm used for fingerprint identification can be used for fingermarks search too; actually, by noting that fingermark minutiae are typically confined to a small area, comparing such a compact set against a full minutiae set characterizing a fingerprint can be viewed as a specific point pattern matching problem, for which optimized approaches can be designed (see for example the method proposed in [27] where the discriminant power of MCC descriptors is exploited to improve a Hough transform-based rigid matcher).

3.3 Segmentation

Separating the print area from the background is very critical in fingermarks, and ad hoc methods are being proposed also according to the background type (see for example [28], where a method is proposed to deal with fingermarks on banknotes).

State-of-the-art fingermark segmentation approaches are based on local total variation [29–31]. For example the model in [30] decomposes a fingermark image into two layers: cartoon and texture. The cartoon layer, consisting of smooth components, contains unwanted components (e.g. structured noise) while the texture layer, which contains the oscillatory or textured component, mainly consists of the fingerprint. This cartoon-texture decomposition facilitates the process of segmentation, as the region of interest can be easily detected from the texture layer using traditional segmentation methods.

A particularly complex case is when two or more fingermarks are partially overlapped and, besides isolating the composite pattern form the background, it is also necessary to separate the pattern into its components [32–34].

3.4 Enhancement

Once the foreground has been segmented, before minutiae can be automatically extracted, the pattern quality needs to be improved. The most effective approaches rely on contextual filtering [16], where the filter characteristics are locally tuned according to the context (i.e. local ridge orientation and local ridge frequency); however when dealing with fingermarks, the context estimation is very critical and inaccurate estimations can compromise the efficacy of the enhancement step.

In [35] a tool for semi-automatic context estimation is proposed. This approach reduces the markup efforts (since the user's input is limited to a few points, see Fig. 3.3), while making the fingermark enhancement quite accurate. However if a fully automatic processing is required, more sophisticated techniques have to be designed. In fact, typical bottom-up context estimation methods (i.e. gradient based approaches for orientations) proved to be ineffective because the noise level can be locally higher than the underlying signal.

Quite recently, some interesting techniques have been introduced based on prior knowledge of fingerprint structure. An off-line learning technique is adopted to determine the space (or dictionary) of feasible context patches, to which each patch in the current fingermark has to be conducted:

- In [36] prior knowledge on ridge-line orientations is represented by means of a dictionary of reference orientation patches. Figure 3.4 shows a flowchart of the proposed algorithm. In the off-line stage, a set of good quality fingerprints is used to construct the dictionary; in the online stage, given a fingermark, its orientations are first estimated using a traditional technique, then corrected by

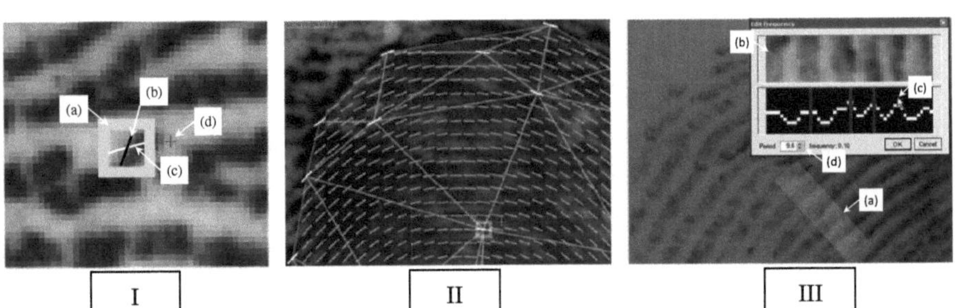

Fig. 3.3 Examples of the user interface proposed in [35] for the markup of the local orientations and frequencies. From *left to right*, **I** manual adjustment of a single local orientation element: (*a*) the selected element, (*b*) the initial orientation proposed by the software, (*c*) the orientation selected by the user moving the mouse cursor (*d*); **II** a larger portion of a fingerprint image shows some local estimations made by the user (*white segments*) and all the local orientations interpolated by the software (*grey segments*); **III** markup of the local frequencies: (*a*) the user clicks on a given location, (*a*) the corresponding oriented window is highlighted on the fingerprint image and (*b*) displayed on a popup window, (*c*) the *grey*-level profile is shown and the users selects some consecutive maxima using the mouse, (*d*) the estimated *ridge-line* frequency and the corresponding period are shown

means of dictionary lookup of orientation patches and compatibility analysis between neighbouring patches.

- [36] proved that the use of prior knowledge (in the form of orientation patch dictionary) is helpful for correcting many errors. However, since the positions of the patches have not been restrained, some orientation patches may occur at impossible locations. For example, the orientation field estimated by this algorithm for the fingermark in Fig. 3.5 contains a wrong delta singularity in the top region, which is not likely to occur in real fingerprints. In [37], Yang et al. propose a robust fingerprint orientation field estimation algorithm, which is based on localized dictionaries of orientation patches. A drawback of localized patches is the need to register the fingerprint with respect to a universal coordinate system; in [37] this is accomplished by a robust registration algorithm

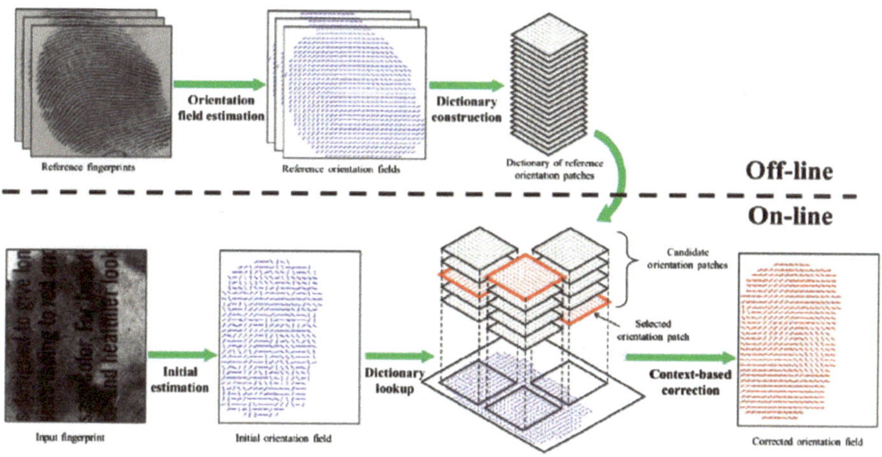

Fig. 3.4 A flowchart of the algorithm proposed in [36]

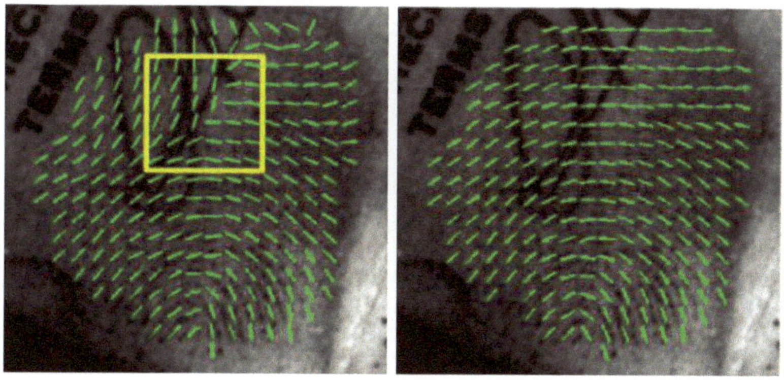

Fig. 3.5 Orientation extraction from a fingermark using the approach proposed in [36] (*on the left*) and in [37] (*on the right*)

based on probabilistic voting of all local orientation patches. The local dictionary approach outperformed the global one in a number of experiments [37] and is currently the best-performing approach in the FvcOnGoing FOE (Fingerprint Orientation Estimation) benchmark [38].

- A limitation of orientation dictionaries is that they cannot provide information about frequency. In [29] a ridge structure dictionary, which is learnt from a set of high quality ridge patches, is then used to restore ridge structure in these patches. Figure 3.6 shows a subset from a dictionary of orientation patches and a subset from a dictionary of ridge structure patches. Experimental results on two fingermark databases (i.e. NIST SD27 and WVU DB) show that the proposed algorithm outperforms previous segmentation and enhancement

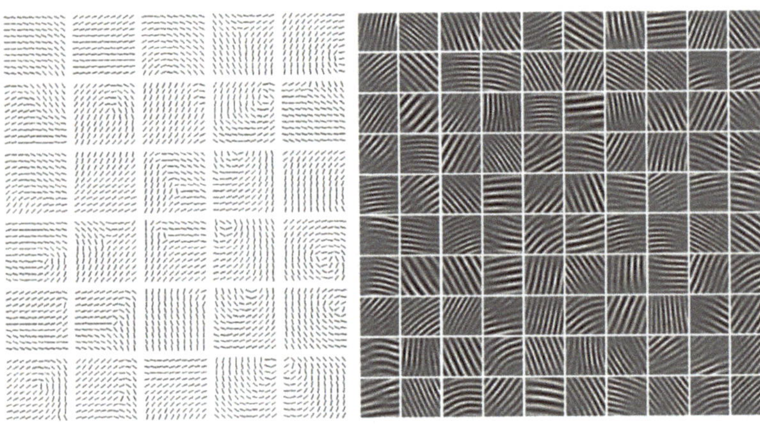

Fig. 3.6 *On the left* A portion of a dictionary of orientation patches; *on the right* a portion of a dictionary of ridge structure patches

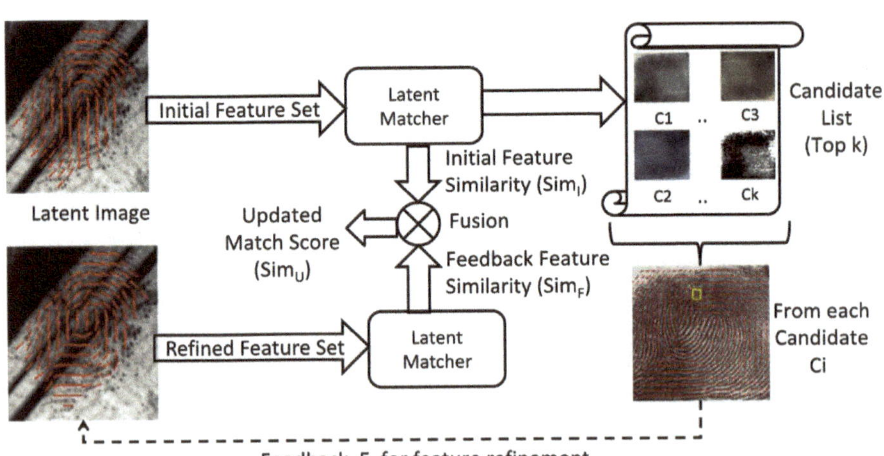

Fig. 3.7 The main steps of the feedback-based feature refinement described in [39]

algorithms and improves the performance of a state-of-the-art commercial fingermark comparison algorithm: in particular, at a rejection rate of 20%, the rank-1 identification rate accuracy increases by 7.43% and 7.23%, respectively, for the NIST SD27 and WVU DB with respect to the baseline performance of a commercial comparison algorithm.

A different approach to get contextual information in a fully automatic manner [39] is relying on the features of the fingerprints in the candidate list to guide the fingermark enhancement and then (re)compare the improved pattern against the candidate list exemplars to consolidate a more reliable score (Fig. 3.7).

3.5 Forensic Applications

This section describes the forensic use of fingerprints and fingermarks within the field of forensic dactyloscopy and details the role of biometric fingerprint recognition technology for both of them.

3.5.1 Applications Using fingerprints

3.5.1.1 Identity Management Within Criminal Justice Systems

Criminal Justice Systems have been forerunners in the adoption of fingerprint recognition technology for the identification and the verification of the identity of criminals, victims and missing persons. AFIS are commonplace in law enforcement since the 1980s to collect and compare fingerprint, and later fingermark specimens [40]. Fingerprint data were first and still are used within Criminal Justice Systems in an identity management perspective, for identity verification as well as closed and open-set identification. It has to be stressed that the reliability of any forensic fingerprint application relies on the integrity of the identity management deployed by the criminal justice systems [41]. The identity infrastructure in place needs to be able to create, challenge and end biometric identities reliably. For example, before the use of biometric solutions in the Dutch prisons, some individuals were serving sentences, substituting themselves to the convicted criminals. Nowadays the Netherlands have implemented, in case of serious crime, a system combining the fingerprint and face modalities to identify and verify that the person behind a claimed identity remains the same along the whole criminal justice chain, from the arrest to the custody to serve the sentence [42].

For the administration of justice it is relevant to reach formal decisions of identity verification or identification. This is only possible if the prior probability of the hypothesis of common source for the test and reference fingerprint specimens can be assigned reliably and if a set of high quality fingerprints (not fingermarks) combined to an accurate biometric technology can provide an overwhelming strength of evidence to support this hypothesis. The availability of secure identity management infrastructures based on the integrity of the fingerprint data and metadata, accurate fingerprint recognition technology and valid inference frameworks are a prerequisite to the forensic use fingerprints and fingermarks within Criminal Justice Systems.

3.5.1.2 Forensic Identification of Missing Persons

The identification of missing persons from a mass disaster depends on the form of this disaster, closed or open. A closed disaster relates to a known number of individuals from a defined group, like an aircraft crash with a passengers list. Open disasters like traffic accidents, natural disasters, technical accidents (fires, explosions), terrorist attacks and events occurring within the context of war relates to an unknown number of individuals from an undefined group [43]. Combinations of these two forms are also conceivable (e.g. aircraft crash in a residential area) [44]. When the prior probabilities can be assigned, the evidential value of the biometric features can be assessed and decision thresholds can be determined. Closed-set identification (1 to N) and open-set identification (1 to N + 1) frameworks apply, respectively, to these two types of disaster. When the prior probabilities cannot be assigned and the decision thresholds cannot be determined, the likelihood ratio inference model (defined hereunder) applies to assess the strength of evidence of the fingermarks and fingerprints [43, 45, 46].

3.5.2 Application Using Fingermarks

3.5.2.1 Forensic Intelligence

Repeat offenders do not only repeat offences but also generally operate according to a similar *modus operandi*, leaving similar traces at different crime scenes. Fingerprint recognition technology can be used to associate fingermarks from different cases to uncover crime phenomena and produce forensic intelligence. For example fingermarks recovered in separate cases can be compared pairwise using fingerprint recognition technology to produce a rank list of N scores, from which a subset of M relevant links from N will be selected (M from N). Comparing fingermarks with fingermarks is scientifically the most challenging application of fingerprint recognition technology to forensic science, due to the limited quality of the specimens compared [47]. For instance the Europol Information System (EIS) is in the process to integrate forensic intelligence capabilities for fingermarks to support the operational activities of the Agency like the fight against illicit drugs, trafficking of human beings or terrorism [43, 48].

3.5.2.2 Forensic Investigation

Even if offenders are aware that they are leaving traces during their criminal activity, large amounts of them are still recovered on crime scenes. That is first of all because it is impossible for a criminal to act without leaving a trace, considering the intensity of the criminal activity as Locard first observed [49]. Traces cannot be avoided due to the physical intensity of criminal activities such as breaking in or killing, but also due to the emotional intensity of the criminal activity. Offenders tend to underestimate, neglect or even forget about the traces they leave, even in meticulously organized and prepared actions like terrorist attacks. For example, how else can we explain the presence of a blue plastic bag containing detonating devices found near the Madrid Atocha train station on 11 March, 2004? It is on this blue plastic bag that one of the most (in)famous fingermarks within the field of forensic dactyloscopy was recovered, developed and submitted for identification. The use of this fingermark to establish who could be a possible suspect in this terrorist attack has demonstrated first during the forensic investigation phase the impressive sensitivity of the AFISs, optimized to minimize the false rejection rate to levels approaching zero, but it has also provided an example of the misuse of this information later during the phase of forensic evaluation.

Because of the large amount of distortion present in the fingermark found on the blue plastic bag and also because of the uncertainty whether it was the result of a single or double imposition (Fig. 3.8b), this fingermark had been initially considered as unusable by the Spanish National Police. This first assessment was later revised and the fingermark was compared with the fingerprint references stored in the Spanish AFIS and shared through Interpol for a search against the 10 billions of fingerprint references (1 billion ten-print cards) stored in the national and immigration fingerprint databases worldwide. And even with a mark of such extreme poor quality, modern systems were able to select a few reference specimens with a surprisingly high degree of similarity with the mark from immense databases. For example, in this case the US Federal Bureau of Investigations (FBI) compared the fingermark with the 700 million reference fingerprints of the criminal master file of the United States Integrated Automated Fingerprint Identification System (US-IAFIS) and established a shortlist of 20 candidates. But the forensic evaluation phase was not performed according to the ACE-V protocol (Analysis, Comparison, Evaluation, Verification), considered as a best practice procedure [50]. The initial examiner failed to conduct a complete analysis of the fingermark before conducting the AFIS search. As a result, three fingermark examiners, two from the FBI and one independent, initially attributed the fingermark developed on the blue plastic bag to an American citizen, Brandon Bieri Mayfield (Fig. 3.8a). The case took an unexpected turn when the Spanish National Police attributed the same mark to an Algerian citizen, Ouhnane Daoud (Fig. 3.8c). Although in casework the ground truth about the origin of a fingermark remains unknown, in this case the FBI withdrew their identification of Mayfield and attributed the fingermark to Ouhnane Daoud. In 2006, the Office of the Inspector General of the US Department of Justice

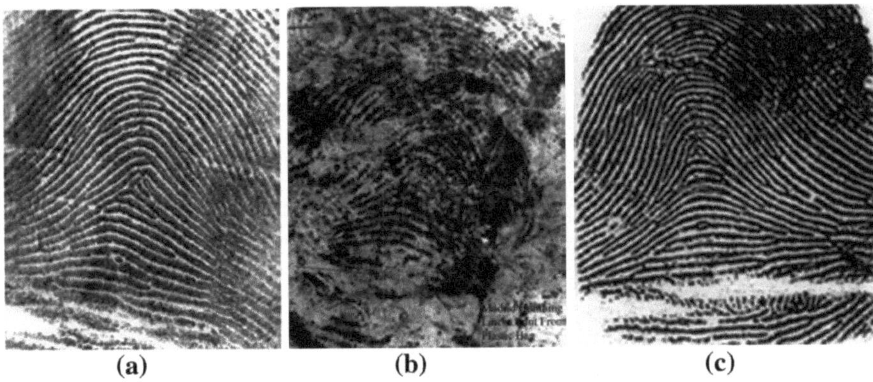

Fig. 3.8 **a** Reference fingerprint of the left index of Brandon Bieri Mayfield [51], **b** fingermark found on a plastic bag containing detonating devices near the Atocha train station, March 11th 2004 [51], **c** reference fingerprint of the right middle finger of Ouhnane Daoud [51]

published a review explaining the reasons for what is considered as an erroneous decision of identification [51].

In their evaluation, the FBI examiners clearly failed to consider some key parameters that govern the search of a poor quality fingermark in an immense database of reference fingerprints during the forensic investigation phase. First, the probability to select reference fingerprints with a very high degree of similarity and minimal differences with the fingermark (and sometimes between them) increases with the size of the database. The forensic practitioners name such pairs of biometric specimens "look alikes". These observations provide the empirical demonstration that the distinctiveness between two specimens (trace and reference) is inherently limited. Second, any forensic investigation procedure leads to the production of a shortlist of reference specimens, but the extreme low quality of a trace increases the probability to shortlist reference specimens with only a limited degree of similarity with the trace. Finally the probability to detect differences between a trace and a reference specimen decreases with their quality, to the point where even qualified and experienced practitioners cannot detect differences of origin.

In these circumstances an erroneous decision of identification may occur, as in the Mayfield case, if the question of the inference of the source of the fingermark is envisaged as a decision based on the criterion of uniqueness. On the other hand, a logical answer can be provided to the court if the answer to the question of the source of the fingermark is envisaged as a measure of distinctiveness leading to the description of the strength of evidence, combined with the explicit estimation of the order of magnitude of the relevant population in the case [52].

Applying such an approach in the Mayfield case, the FBI examiners would have noticed that the size of the relevant population that can be estimated (considering that the fingermark has been recovered in Madrid, Spain and the suspected person was living in Portland, Oregon USA) is superior by several orders of magnitude to the strength of evidence that can be assigned on the basis of the observations made on the fingermark (Fig. 3.8b) and the fingerprint (Fig. 3.8a), making their decision of identification unlikely to be correct.

3.5.2.3 Forensic Evaluation

The example of the Mayfield case demonstrates that the crucial challenge of forensic evaluation consists in assigning or computing the most correct (and not the biggest) strength of evidence, on basis of the observations made on a pair of fingermark and fingerprint specimens. Human-based and computer-assisted methods using fingerprint recognition technology have been developed to assign or compute the strength of evidence. Both approaches rely on the Bayes theorem of conditional probabilities to express the strength of evidence in the form a likelihood ratio (LR) in a uniform framework [53]. This framework is considered as logical and balanced and the LR can be considered as the metric describing the strength of evidence [54].

At source level, the LR is defined as the ratio of the probability of the observations (evidence E) in the light of a pair of mutually exclusive alternative hypotheses as follows: hypothesis H1—the two specimens originate from a common source and hypothesis H2—the two specimens originate from different sources. Generally, hypothesis H1, stating that the trace material originates from the suspected person, is supported by the prosecution. Hypothesis H2, stating that the trace material originates from another individual randomly chosen within the relevant population of potential sources of the trace, is supported by the defence.

The strength of evidence is assigned or computed as the ratio of two probabilities: the probability of the evidence when the prosecution hypothesis is true when divided by the probability of the evidence when the defence hypothesis is true. In the Eq. (2), I represents the relevant background information about the case, for instance the selection process of the suspected person and the nature of the relevant population [52]. The result, expressed as a likelihood ratio, is calculated as follows:

$$\underset{\substack{\text{Posterior}\\ \text{probaility}\\ \text{ratio}}}{\frac{P(H_1|E,I)}{Pk(H_2|E,I)}} = \underset{\substack{\text{Likelihood}\\ \text{ration}}}{\frac{P(E|H_1,I)}{P(E|H_2,I)}} * \underset{\substack{\text{Prior}\\ \text{probability}\\ \text{ratio}}}{\frac{P(H_1,I)}{P(H_2,I)}} \tag{2}$$

The posterior probability ratio is calculated as the multiplication of the prior probability ratio by the likelihood ratio. The role of the forensic practitioner is limited to the assessment of the likelihood ratio. The duty to provide the prior probability ratio and to make decisions on basis of the posterior probability ratio remains to the trier of fact [43].

Human-based methods rely on forensic practitioners using knowledge and experience to assign the LR on basis of their personal probabilities. On the other hand, computer-assisted methods and LR-based systems rely on statistical

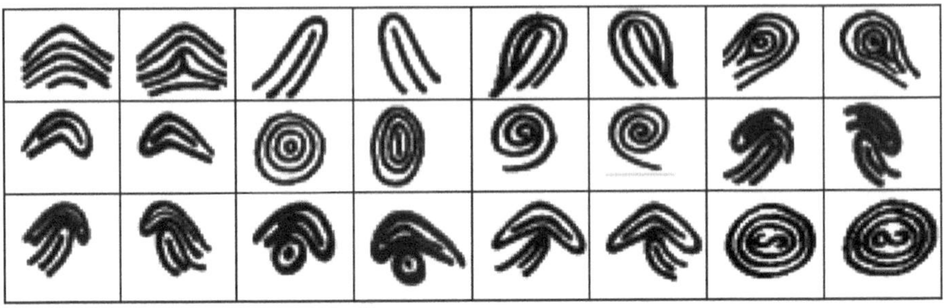

Fig. 3.9 Extended set of fingerprint general patterns (Courtesy from Arent de Jongh and Anko Lubach, Netherlands Forensic Institute)

probabilities obtained from the combination of databases and fingerprint recognition technology to compute the LR. The strength of a LR-based system is to provide statistical probabilities on the set of distinctive features that can be extracted automatically. The strength of human beings is to also to be able to consider features that cannot be handled by biometric technology yet, like an extended set of general pattern in fingermarks (Fig. 3.9). Statistical probabilities are considered as more objective and personal probabilities more subjective.

The classical "forensic identification" disciplines relying mainly on personal probabilities for the assessment of the evidence are being increasingly challenged [55], especially because of the development of evidence based on DNA profiles governed by statistical data and the evolving requirements for the admissibility of evidence following the Daubert decision by the Supreme Court of the USA [52]. The quality of the inference provided by computer-assisted LR-based systems strongly depends on the quantity and properties of the data used to estimate the intravariability/within-source variability and the intervariability/between-source variability [56]. The LR approach has been first implemented for the DNA modality [53]. Since then numerous computer-assisted methods have been proposed to compute LRs for different biometric modalities, and among them fingermarks [57].

The current methods described in the literature can be classified as feature-based (Fig. 3.10) [58] or score-based approaches (Fig. 3.11) [59]. When a limited number of features are extracted from each specimen, the model parameters can be estimated with a limited amount of data [60]. Such an approach is feature-based; it involves statistical modelling at the level of the features, using for example probability density functions under the two alternative hypotheses to produce the LR values. When a large number of features are extracted from each specimen, score-based methods are frequently used as a way to reduce the multidimensionality of the feature space and to estimate the model parameters in one dimension [61]. The LR values computed from comparison scores are typically the result of a comparison performed by pattern recognition and machine-learning algorithms [62].

Ongoing discussions are taking place within the forensic community about the scientific merits and flaws of these approaches and about the challenges that represent their implementation in practical systems [63–65].

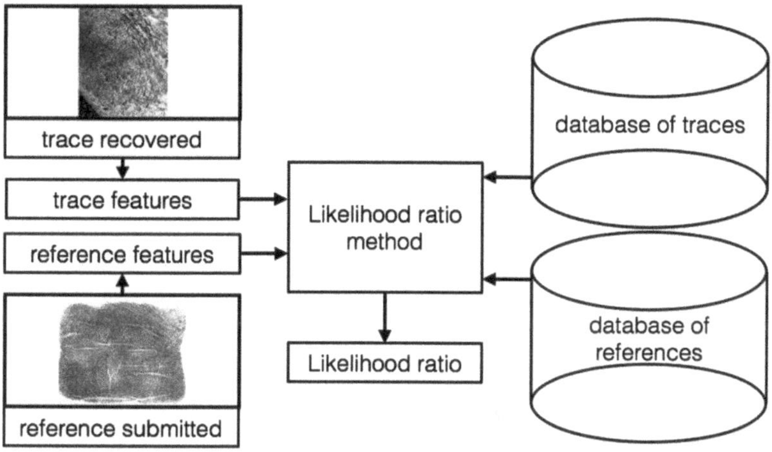

Fig. 3.10 Framework for a feature-based LR computation

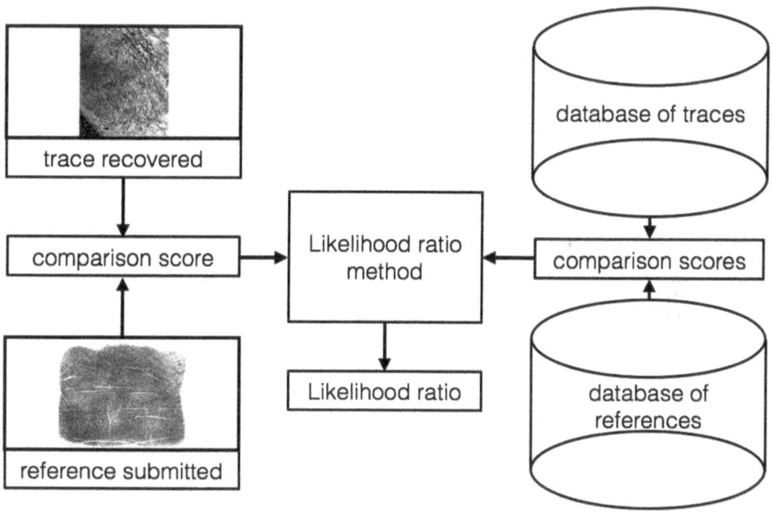

Fig. 3.11 Framework for a score-based LR computation

3.5.3 Current Challenges

3.5.3.1 Automation and Transparency

In forensic applications, the feature extraction from poor quality fingerprint and fingermark images remains a computer-assisted process, combining the performance of the subjective and somehow inconsistent ability of humans to the more objective but also more limited performance of computers for some complex pattern recognition tasks. Both the human inconsistencies and the limits of the computer affect the performance of the feature extraction and, as a consequence, the performance of the forensic processes based on the use of fingermarks and fingerprints. In the future, a feature extraction process at once reliable and completely automated (lights-out-mode) is desirable. Steps in this direction can be done, not only by refining the minutiae extraction process, but also by enriching the feature vector with other available, measurable, discriminatory, permanent and robust features, for e.g. the extended set of fingerprint general patterns (see above) or the generalization of the use of the number of ridges between the minutiae [40].

Fingerprint practitioners need a better understanding of the functioning of the fingerprint recognition technology implemented in the AFISs in order to operate AFIS processes in a more transparent manner. In absence of an authoritative source to help them interpret the AFIS results, they can only speculate about how the core algorithms are designed and what could influence their output. This is not without raising difficulties for the practitioners to be accountable for results driven by the technology [40, 66].

3.5.3.2 Scalability and Interoperability

The scalability of the paper-based ten-print collections was limited by the necessary trade-off between selectivity and reliability imposed by manual classification systems, and the coexistence of several paper-based systems around the world limited their interoperability at an international level. The implementation of Automated Fingerprint Identification Systems solved the problem of scalability for the national fingerprint databases, but the interoperability problem remains as the first generations of AFIS incorporated feature vectors that are encoded using proprietary formats [40]. Currently, the problem of interoperability between different types of AFISs is on the way to be solved partially by the widespread use of the ANSI-NIST biometric exchange file format, but the predominant use of proprietary formats for the feature vectors remains. This improvement opens a new opportunity in terms of scalability, with the possibility to extend the interoperability of the AFISs at a global level and to integrate the AFIS functionality into a broader platform for multimodal biometric identification, for example including facial recognition, speech and DNA [40]. But this opportunity also raises the challenge of merging the results from the different biometric modalities using fusion strategies adapted to the different forensic applications: forensic identification (decision), forensic investigation and intelligence (selection) and forensic evaluation (description) [43].

3.5.3.3 Forensic Fingermark Processes

In forensic investigation and intelligence processes, the short lists of potential sources still predominantly have a fixed size based on the rank information provided by the AFISs. The efficiency of these processes would largely benefit from lists of variable size, combining the information of the rank and score value to output a description of the strength of the link made between the fingermark and the reference fingerprints [40].

Forensic evaluation of fingermarks and fingerprints consists mainly in the inference of identity of the source of a fingermark and a fingerprint. Currently, this task remains mainly performed by fingermark examiners. They apply the Analysis, Comparison, Evaluation, Verification (ACE-V) procedure and, in some countries, a numerical standard, to substantiate three types of qualitative opinions: identification, exclusion or inconclusive. As their evaluation is deterministic, fingermark examiners also make an implicit use of their own subjective probabilities of the rarity of the features used for identification. They refine these subjective probabilities through training and experience [40, 50].

In forensic research, the inference of identity of the source of a fingermark and a fingerprint is also envisaged, combining statistical models, digitized fingerprint and fingermark databases as well as a scientific methodology; namely the likelihood ratio approach based on Bayes' theorem. This approach aims to offer a uniform framework and a transparent methodology to fingermark examiners, and to assist them in producing a logical, testable and quantitative evaluation of fingerprint evidence [67]. Prototypes for forensic fingermark evaluation exist and some rely on fingerprint biometric technology. But their validation, including criteria about the robustness of the underlying assumptions and criteria about the precision, the accuracy and the calibration of the results is a critical step prior to their acceptance by the fingerprint scientific and legal communities [68].

3.6 Conclusion

This chapter introduced the use of AFIS for ID verification, identification, forensic investigation and intelligence. These systems have greatly improved the operational productivity of law enforcement agencies and reduced the cost of hiring and training human fingerprint experts. In about fifty years they evolved from initial prototypes to powerful systems, able to process millions identification requests per second. Scientific research in fingerprint recognition and fingermark processing is still very active; among the various recent interesting developments, it is worth mentioning:

- an extremely efficient fingerprint comparison algorithm, which exploits GPUs to achieve a throughput of millions of comparisons per second on a simple PC;
- the availability of tools for semi-automatic feature markup for the enhancement of fingermarks;
- learning-based techniques for fingermark processing, which exploits prior knowledge of fingerprint structure to improve the quality of automatically extracted features.

All the forensic applications have benefited from the improvements offered by the fingerprint biometric technology in terms automation and performance. Automatic fingerprint identification systems are currently an integral part of the different forensic processes: identification, intelligence, investigation and evaluation. But if the contribution of the fingerprint biometric technology is essential in the good execution of the operational forensic processes, several challenges remain:

- First, the extraction of features from poor quality fingerprint and fingermark images is still a computer-assisted process, when full automation (lights-out-mode) is desirable.
- Second, increasing the transparency of the fingerprint biometric technology would help the practitioners to interpret the AFIS results.
- Third, cooperation, harmonization and standardization have enabled for an improvement gap of the fingerprint biometric technology. This technological improvement still has to reverberate operationally in order for the forensic processes to become fully scalable and interoperable in practice.
- Finally the fingerprint biometric technology has opened the door to render the fingermark evaluation, in particular, more objective, but a long research, validation and education effort is still necessary to achieve its implementation and to gain the acceptance of the fingerprint scientific and legal communities.

References

1. Lee HC, Gaensslen RE (2001) Advances in fingerprint technology. Elsevier Publishing, New York
2. Meuwly D (2015) Forensic use of fingermarks and fingerprints. In: Stan Z., Jain, AL (eds) Encyclopedia of biometrics, 2nd edn. Springer
3. Federal Bureau of Investigation (1984) The Science of fingerprints: classification and uses. Federal Bureau of Investigation, Government Publication, Washington, DC, US
4. Federal Bureau of Investigation (1991) The FBI fingerprint identification automation program: issues and options. Federal Bureau of Investigation, Government Publication, Washington, DC, US
5. Moses KR, Higgins P, McCabe M, Prabhakar S, Swann S (2011) Automated fingerprint identification system (AFIS). In: SWGFAST—the fingerprint sourcebook, scientific working group on friction ridge analysis study and technology and national institute of Justice, pp 1–33
6. Wegstein JH, Rafferty JF, Pencak WJ (1968) Matching fingerprints by computer, National Bureau of Standards, U.S. Department of Commerce, Washington, DC, Technical Note 466
7. Wegstein JH (1969) A computer oriented single-fingerprint identification system, National Bureau of Standards, U.S. Department of Commerce, Washington, DC, Technical Note 443 1969
8. Wegstein JH (1970) Automated fingerprint identification, National Bureau of Standards, U.S. Department of Commerce, Washington, DC, Technical Note 538
9. Wegstein JH (1972) Manual and automated fingerprint registration, National Bureau of Standards, U.S. Department of Commerce, Washington, DC, NBS Technical Note 730
10. Wegstein JH (1972) The M40 fingerprint matcher, National Bureau of Standards, U.S. Department of Commerce, Washington, DC, Technical Note 878

11. Wegstein JH, Rafferty JF (1978) The LX39 latent fingerprint matcher, National Bureau of Standards, U.S. Department of Commerce, Washington, DC, Special Publication 500–536
12. Wegstein JH, Rafferty JF (1979) The automated identification of fingerprints. In: Dermatoglyphics—fifty years later, Washington, DC
13. Wegstein JH (1982) An automated fingerprint identification system, National Bureau of Standards, U.S. Department of Commerce, Washington, DC, NBS Special Publication 500–589
14. Stoney DA (1991) What made us ever think we could individualize using statistics. J Foren Sci Soc 31(2)
15. Watson CI et al (2015) Fingerprint vendor technology evaluation 2012, NIST, NIST Interagency/Internal Report (NISTIR)—8034
16. Maltoni D, Maio D, Jain AK, Prabhakar S (2009) Handbook of fingerprint recognition, 2nd edn. Springer, New York, NJ, USA
17. FBI—CJIS division (1999) Electronic fingerprint transmission specification, FBI, CJIS-RS-0010 (V7)
18. Indovina M, Hicklin RA, Kiebuzinski GI (2011) ELFT-EFS evaluation of latent fingerprint technologies: extended feature sets (Evaluation 1), National Institute of Standards and Technology, US Department of Commerce, NISTIR 7775
19. Indovina MD, Dvornychenko V, Hicklin RA, Kiebuzinski GI (2012) ELFT-EFS evaluation of latent fingerprint technologies: extended feature sets (Evaluation 2), National Institute of Standards and Technology, US Department of Commerce, NISTIR 7859
20. Jain AK, Feng J (2011) Latent fingerprint matching. IEEE Trans Pattern Anal Mach Intell 33 (1):88–100
21. Zhao Q, Jain AK (2010) On the utility of extended fingerprint features: a study on pores. In: CVPR workshop on biometrics, San Francisco
22. Cappelli R, Ferrara M, Maltoni D (2010) Minutia Cylinder-Code: a new representation and matching technique for fingerprint recognition. IEEE Trans Pattern Anal Mach Intell 32 (12):2128–2141
23. Cappelli R, Ferrara M, Maio D (2012) A fast and accurate palmprint recognition system based on minutiae. IEEE Trans Syst Man Cybern Part B 42(3):956–962
24. Cappelli R, Ferrara M, Maltoni D (2011) Fingerprint Indexing based on minutia cylinder code. IEEE Trans Pattern Anal Mach Intell 33(5):1051–1057
25. Cappelli R, Ferrara M, Maltoni D, Tistarelli M (2010) MCC: a baseline algorithm for fingerprint verification in FVC-onGoing. In: Proceedings 11th international conference on control, automation, robotics and vision (ICARCV), Singapore
26. Cappelli R, Ferrara M, Maltoni D (2015) Large-scale fingerprint identification on GPU. Inf Sci 306:1–20
27. Paulino AA, Feng J, Jain AK (2013) Latent fingerprint matching using descriptor-based hough transform. IEEE Trans Inf Forensics Secur 8(1):31–45
28. Si X, Feng J, Zhou J (2014) Enhancing latent fingerprints on banknotes. In: IEEE international joint conference on biometrics, Clearwater, FL, USA, pp 1–8
29. Cao K, Liu E, Jain AK (2014) Segmentation and enhancement of latent fingerprints: a coarse to fine ridge structure dictionary. IEEE Trans Pattern Anal Mach Intell 36(9):1847–1859
30. Zhang J, Lai R, Kuo C-CJ (2013) Adaptive directional total-variation model for latent fingerprint segmentation. IEEE Trans Inf Forensics Secur 8(8):1261–1273
31. Choi H, Boaventura M, Boaventura IAG, Jain AK (2012) Automatic segmentation of latent fingerprints. In: IEEE fifth international conference on biometrics: theory, applications, Arlington, VA, USA, pp 303–310
32. Zhao Q, Jain AK (2012) Model based separation of overlapping latent fingerprints. IEEE Trans Inf Forensics Secur 7(3):904–918
33. Zhang N, Zang Y, Yang X, Jia X, Tian J (2014) Adaptive orientation model fitting for latent overlapped fingerprints separation. IEEE Trans Inf Forensics Secur 9(10):1547–1556
34. Feng J, Shi Y, Zhou J (2012) Robust and efficient algorithms for separating latent overlapped fingerprints. IEEE Trans Inf Forensics Secur 7(5):1498–1510

35. Cappelli R, Maio D, Maltoni D (2009) Semi-automatic enhancement of very low quality fingerprint. In: 6th international symposium on image and signal processing and analysis (ISPA09), Salzburg, pp 678–683
36. Feng J, Zhou J, Jain AK (2013) Orientation field estimation for latent fingerprint enhancement. IEEE Trans Pattern Anal Mach Intell 35(4):925–940
37. Yang X, Feng J, Zhou J (2014) Localized dictionaries based orientation field estimation for latent fingerprints. IEEE Trans Pattern Anal Mach Intell 36(5):955–969
38. BioLab. (2015) FVC-onGoing web site. http://biolab.csr.unibo.it/fvcongoing
39. Arora SS, Liu E, Cao K, Jain AK (2014) Latent fingerprint matching: performance gain via feedback from exemplar prints. IEEE Trans Pattern Anal Mach Intell 36(12):2452–2465
40. Meuwly D (2014) Friction ridge skin—AFIS. In: Jamieson A, Moenssens A (eds) Encyclopedia of forensic science, Chichester, UK. Wiley
41. Meuwly D (2010) ID management in 2020, ID.academy. The Hague
42. Plomp MGA, Grijpink JHAM (2011) Combating identity fraud in the public domain: information strategies for healthcare and criminal justice. In Proceedings of the 11th European conference on e-government, Ljubljana, Slovenia
43. Meuwly D, Veldhuis R (2012) Forensic biometrics: from two communities to one discipline. In: 2012 BIOSIG-proceedings of the international conference of the biometrics special interest group (BIOSIG), pp 207–218
44. Interpol (2009) Disaster victims identification guide. Interpol, Lyon
45. Biedermann A, Taroni F, Margot P (2012) Reply to Budowle, Ge, Chakraborty and Gill-King: use of prior odds for missing persons identifications. Investig Genet 3:1–2
46. Budowle B, Ge J, Chakraborty R, Gill-King H (2011) Use of prior odds for missing persons identifications. Investig Genet 2:1–6
47. Ribaux O, Walsh SJ, Margot P (2006) The contribution of forensic science to crime analysis and investigation: forensic intelligence. Forensic Sci Int 156:171–181
48. Europol (2011) Europol information management: products and services. Europol, The Hague
49. Locard E (1920) L'enquête criminelle et les méthodes scientifiques. Ernst Flammarion, Paris
50. Langenburg GM (2012) A critical analysis and study of the ACE-V process, University of Lausanne, Switzerland, PhD thesis
51. Fine GE (2006) A review of the FBI's handling of the Brandon Mayfield case, Office of the Inspector General, U.S. Department of Justice
52. Dessimoz D, Champod C (2008) Linkages between biometrics and forensic science. In: Handbook of biometrics. Springer, pp. 425–459
53. Evett I (1998) Towards a uniform framework for reporting opinions in forensic science casework. Sci Justice 38(3):198–202
54. Good IJ (1991) Weight of evidence and the Bayesian likelihood ratio. In: Aitken CGG, Stoney DA (eds) The use of statistics in forensic science. Ellis Horwood, Chichester UK, pp 85–106
55. Saks M, Koehler J (2005) The coming paradigm shift in forensic identification science. Science 309(5736):892–895
56. Meuwly D (2006) Forensic individualisation from biometric data. Sci Justice 46(4):205–213
57. Neumann C et al (2006) Computation of likelihood ratios in fingerprint identification for configurations of three minutiae. J Forensic Sci 51(6):1255–1266
58. Lindley DV (1977) A problem in forensic science. Biometrika 64(2):207–213
59. Van Leeuwen DA, Brümmer N (2007) An introduction to application-independent evaluation of speaker recognition systems. In: Speaker classification I. Springer, pp 330–353
60. Bolck A, Weyermann C, Dujourdy L, Esseiva P, van den Berg J (2009) Different likelihood ratio approaches to evaluate the strength of evidence of MDMA tablet comparisons. Forensic Sci Int 191(1):42–51
61. Gonzalez-Rodriguez J, Drygajlo A, Ramos-Castro D, Garcia-Gomar M, Ortega-Garcia J (2006) Robust estimation, interpretation and assessment of likelihood ratios in forensic speaker recognition. Comput Speech Lang 20(2):331–355

62. Jain A, Ross A (2015) Bridging the gap: from biometrics to forensics. In: Philosoph Trans Roy Soc B Biol Sci 370(1674)
63. Alberink I, de Jongh A (2015) Authors' Response. J Forensic Sci 60(1):257–258
64. Alberink I, de Jongh A, Rodriguez C (2014) Fingermark evidence evaluation based on automated fingerprint identification system matching scores: the effect of different types of conditioning on likelihood ratios. J Forensic Sci 59(1):70–81
65. Neumann C, Saunders CP (2014) Commentary on: Alberink I, de Jongh A, Rodriguez C. Fingermark evidence evaluation based on automated fingerprint identification system matching scores: the effect of different types of conditioning on likelihood ratios. J Forensic Sci 59(1):70–81
66. Smith ML, Noorman ME, Martin AK (2010) Automating the public sector and organizing accountabilities. Commun Assoc Inf Syst 26(1)
67. Neumann C, Evett IW, Skerrett J (2012) Quantifying the weight of evidence from a forensic fingerprint comparison: a new paradigm. J Roy Stat Soc: Ser A (Stat Soc) 175(2):371–415
68. Neumann C (2012) Statistics and probabilities as a means to support fingerprint examination. In: Ramotowski R (ed) Lee and Gaensslen's advances in fingerprint technology. CRC Press, pp 419–466
69. Lindoso A, Entrena L, Izquierdo J (2007) FPGA-based acceleration of fingerprint minutiae matching. In: 2007 3rd southern conference on programmable logic, 2007. SPL'07, Mar del Plata, Argentina, pp 81–86
70. Jiang RM, Crookes D (2008) FPGA-based minutia matching for biometric fingerprint image database retrieval. J Real-Time Image Proc 3(3):177–182
71. Peralta D, Triguero I, Sanchez-Reillo R, Herrera F, Benitez JM (2014) Fast fingerprint identification for large databases. Pattern Recogn 47(2):588–602
72. Gutierrez PD, Lastra M, Herrera F, Benitez JM (2014) A high performance fingerprint matching system for large databases based on GPU. IEEE Trans Inf Forensics Secur 9(1): 62–71

Chapter 4
Challenges for Fingerprint Recognition—Spoofing, Skin Diseases, and Environmental Effects

Is Fingerprint Recognition Really so Reliable and Secure?

Martin Drahanský, Ondřej Kanich and Eva Březinová

Abstract This chapter tries to find answers to the questions whether the fingerprint recognition is really so reliable and secure. The most biometric systems based on fingerprint recognition have very low error rates, but are these error rates really telling us everything about the quality of such a biometric system? What happens when we use spoofs to deceive the biometric system? What happens when the genuine user has any kind of skin disease on his fingertips? And could we acquire a fingerprint with acceptable quality if there are some distortions on a finger or there are some environmental effects influencing the scanning technology? Reading this chapter brings you an introduction of preparation of finger fakes (spoofs), spoof detection methods, summarization of skin diseases and their influence on papillary lines, and finally the environmental effects are discussed at the end.

4.1 Spoofing and Anti-spoofing

The first subchapter starts with spoofing and anti-spoofing techniques for fingerprint recognition systems. It means that we try to use any kind of finger fake or dead real finger to get an unauthorized access to a biometric system. When a genuine user has already registered his finger in a fingerprint recognition system, there are still several ways how to deceive the biometric system. In order to deceive the

M. Drahanský (✉) · O. Kanich
Brno University of Technology, Faculty of Information Technology,
Brno, Czech Republic
e-mail: drahan@fit.vutbr.cz

E. Březinová
1st Department of Dermatovenereology, St. Anne's University Hospital,
Faculty of Medicine & Masaryk University, Brno, Czech Republic

M. Tistarelli and C. Champod (eds.), *Handbook of Biometrics for Forensic Science*, Advances in Computer Vision and Pattern Recognition,
DOI 10.1007/978-3-319-50673-9_4

fingerprint system, an attacker may put the following objects on the fingerprint scanner [1, 3]:

- *Registered* (enrolled) *finger*. The highest risk is that a legitimate user is forced, e.g., by an armed criminal, to put his live finger on the scanner under duress. Another risk is that a genuine user is compelled to fall asleep with a sleeping drug in order to make free use of his live finger.
- *Unregistered finger* (an impostor's attempt). An attack against a biometric system by an impostor (not necessary an attacker—this could be only an inquisitive person) with his own biometric characteristic is referred as a non-effort forgery.
- *Severed fingerprint of enrolled finger*. A reprehensible attack may be performed using the finger severed from the hand of a genuine user, registered in the biometric system. This kind of attack could be done on a living user or dead user. In both cases, the finger could be used for a limited time only. After several hours, the fingerprint is very often in so bad condition that no papillary lines could be acquired.
- *Genetic clone of enrolled finger*. It should be stated that monozygotic twins do not have the same fingerprint, and the same will be very probably true for clones [10]. The reason is that fingerprints are not entirely determined only genetically but rather by the pattern of nerve growth in the skin. Furthermore, different intrauterine pressures in mother's uterus play an important role in creation of the fingerprint global structure (class) of the fingerprint. It means that such pattern is not exactly the same even for identical twins.
- *Artificial clone of enrolled finger*. More probable attacks against fingerprint systems may use an artificial finger. An artificial finger can be produced from a printed fingerprint made by a copy machine or a graphical processing technique in the same way as forged documents. If an attacker can make then a mold of the enrolled finger by directly modeling it, he can finally also make an artificial finger from a suitable material (see examples in this subchapter). He may also make a mold of the enrolled finger by making a 3D model based on its residual fingerprint.
- *Others*. In some fingerprint systems, an error in authentication may be caused by making noise or flashing a light against the fingerprint scanner, or by heating up, cooling down, humidifying, impacting on, or vibrating the scanner outside its environmental tolerances. We will discuss some of these factors in the third subchapter.

There are possible attacks on algorithms, data transport, and hardware, but these kinds of attacks are out of scope of this subchapter. We will discuss attack possibilities on the input device—fingerprint scanner. One of the simplest possibilities is to produce an artificial finger(print) using soft silicon, gummy and plastic material, or similar substances [10, 18]—see the later part of this subchapter. The fingerprint of a person enrolled in a database is easy to acquire, even without the user's cooperation. Latent fingerprints on daily-use products or on sensors of the access control system itself may be used as templates. To discourage potential attackers from presenting a fake finger (i.e., an imitation of the fingertip and the papillary lines) or, even worse, to hurt a person to gain access, the system must be augmented by an anti-spoofing component [3]. To prevent false acceptance we have to recognize whether the finger on the plate of the fingerprint sensor (also referred to as fingerprint scanner) is alive or not. First of all, we will introduce anti-spoofing techniques (often called liveness detection methods), which are based on various principles. Their purpose is to detect whether the presented finger is alive (and simultaneously the fingerprint is acquired) or any kind of finger(print) spoof is used.

4.1.1 Perspiration

This software-based method processes the information already acquired by a fingerprint scanner—the principle of this technique is the detection of perspiration as an indication of liveness (see Fig. 4.1) [17]. It is worth noting that the outmost layer of the human skin contains around 600 till 1,000 sweat glands per square inch [17] —this amount changes according to the position of skin on the body. These sweat glands diffuse sweat (a dilute sodium chloride solution) on to the surface of skin through pores. The position of skin pores does not change over time and their pore-to-pore distance is approximately 0.5 mm over fingertips [17].

The perspiration method is based on a high difference in the dielectric constant and electrical conductivity between the drier lipids that constitute the outer layer of the skin and the moister sweaty areas near the perspiring pores. The dielectric constant of sweat is around 30 times higher than the lipid.

4.1.2 Spectroscopic Characteristics

This hardware-based method may be regarded not only as an anti-spoofing mechanism but also as an individual biometric system with an inherent anti-spoofing capability.

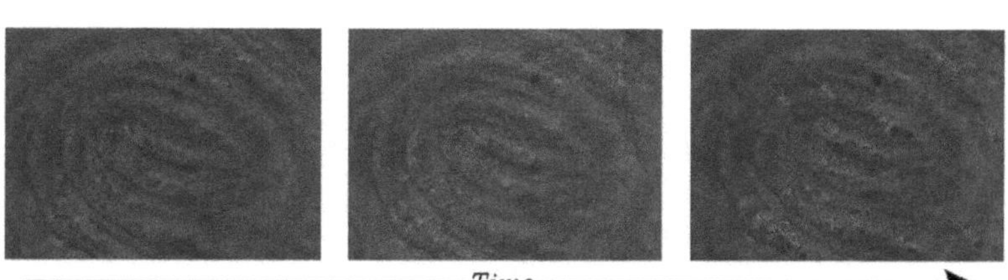

Fig. 4.1 Ascent of sweat from sweat pores on a fingertip (4 × zoomed)

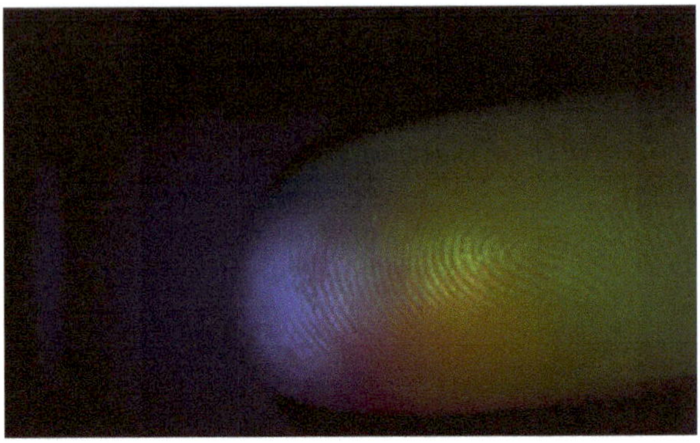

Fig. 4.2 Merge of original fingerprint images illuminated by various wavelengths in RGB [13]

Living human skin has certain unique optical characteristics due to its chemical composition, which predominately affects optical absorbance properties, as well as its multilayered structure, which has a significant effect on the resulting scattering properties [16]. When collecting images generated from different illumination wavelengths sent into the skin, different subsurface skin features may be measured and used to ensure that the material is a living human skin. When such a multi-spectral sensor is combined with a conventional fingerprint reader, the resulting sensing system can provide a high level of certainty that the fingerprint originates from a living finger. The principle of this technique lies in passing light of different wavelengths through a sample and measuring the light returned, which is affected by the structural and chemical properties of the sample. Figure 4.2 shows the color image obtained from a finger illuminated by light with various wavelengths and by merging the original images in RGB color model to one final image.

4.1.3 Ultrasonic Technology

General ultrasonic method [10] uses a transmitter, which emits acoustic signals toward the fingerprint, and a receiver, which detects the echo signals affected by the interaction with the fingerprint—very often transmitter and receiver are combined into one unit called transceiver. A receiver utilizes the fact that ridges (skin) and valleys (air) have difference in acoustic impedance, therefore the echo signals are reflected and diffracted differently in the contact area. This approach with inherent anti-spoof testing capability among its foremost principles uses the fact that sound waves are not only reflected and diffracted, but are also subject to some additional scattering and transformation. This phenomenon is called contact scattering [10] and it was discovered that this scattering is, to a significant extent, affected by the subsurface structure of the acquired object. Hence, the class corresponding to the live tissue could be modeled and whenever the received acoustic waves are inconsistent with this class, they are rejected. The main problem here is not to obtain clear signals, but to analyze and to make a reconstruction of internal structures from signals, which are very difficult to interpret.

4.1.4 Physical Characteristics: Temperature

This simple method measures the temperature of epidermis during a fingerprint acquisition. The temperature of human epidermis of a finger lies in the range of approximately 25–37°C (see examples in Fig. 4.3). However, this range usually has to be wider to make the system usable under different conditions. In addition, there are many people who have distortions in blood circulation, i.e., a fact which leads to deviations in the body temperature and hence to wrong anti-spoof module decision.

4.1.5 Physical Characteristics: Hot and Cold Stimulus

This technique is based on the fact that the human finger reacts differently to thermal stimuli compared with other artificial (nonliving) material.

The designed anti-spoofing testing module [19] works as follows. A stimulus-giving section gives a stimulus (it may cover cool and hot stimulus) to the finger by a contact plate with which the finger makes contact. Next, typical information could be measured by an organism information-measuring section, which is produced by the live finger in response to the stimulus. Concretely, the amount of the fluctuation for the flow rate of the blood flowing in the peripheral vascular tracts varies according to the stimuli. Hence, as peripheral vascular tracts of the fingertip are extended or contracted, the amplitude value of the blood flow is measured and processed by an organism information-measuring section. Under hot stimulus the amplitude of the blood flow increases, while it decreases under cold stimulus. Moreover, according to the autonomic nervous system, the amplitude is delayed a

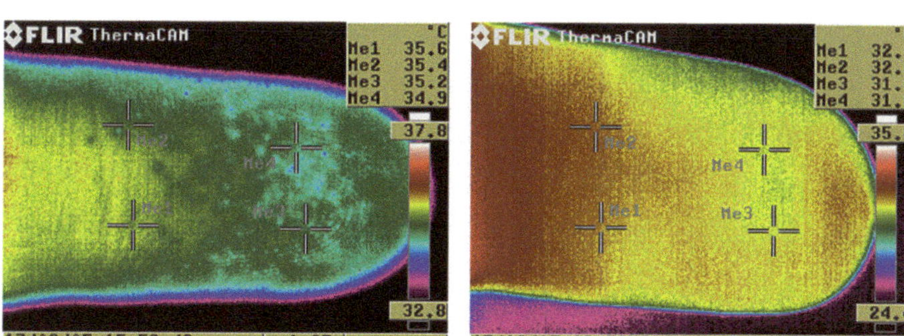

Fig. 4.3 Thermo-scans of fingertips acquired using a thermo-camera FLIR

little with respect to the application of the stimulus. Since these facts are typically observed when the live fingers are measured, they could be employed to distinguish live among artificial and dead samples.

4.1.6 Physical Characteristics: Pressure Stimulus

The principle of this method lies in concrete changes in characteristics of the live skin, which are realized due to pressure applied to the finger [11]. Since the structure and the characteristics of artificial and dead samples are different, when compared with a live finger, this phenomenon could not be seen if such samples were used.

The color of the live skin of the finger without pressure is usually reddish, but becomes whitish when pressure is applied to the skin of the finger. Hence, for the purposes of the device it is suitable to measure the spectral reflectance in the blue and green spectral range (see Fig. 4.4). The difference (in RGB model) between average R values is approximately 11, in G approximately 42, and in B approximately 20 [11].

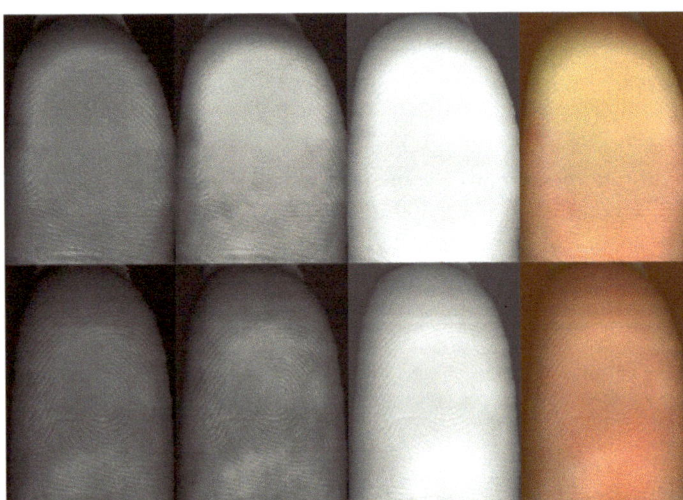

Fig. 4.4 Comparison of pressed finger (*1st row*) and non-pressed finger (*2nd row*). In the *1st column* (from the *left*), there is only the R-channel, the G-channel is in the *2nd column*, the B-channel is in the *3rd column* and in the *4th channel* there is the finger in all RGB colors [11]

4.1.7 Physical Characteristics: Electrical Properties

Some anti-spoofing methods are based on the fact that the live human skin has different electrical properties compared with other materials [10, 14]. The suitable fingerprint recognition system could be extended by an electrode system and an electrical evaluation unit.

The *conductivity* [10] of the human skin is based on humidity, which is dependent on people's biological characteristics and environmental conditions: some people have dry fingers and others have sweaty (wet) ones; also during different seasons, climatic, and environmental conditions, humidity differs significantly. As a result, the span of permissible resistance levels has to be big enough to make the system usable. In such a situation it is quite easy for an impostor to fool the system.

The *relative dielectric constant* (RDC) [10] of a specific material reflects the extent to which it concentrates the electrostatic lines of flux. Many advocates claim that the RDC has the ability to distinguish between real and artificial samples. However, the RDC is highly dependent on the humidity of the sample, so the same situation as in the case of conductivity arises. To fool this method, an attacker can simply use an artificial sample and dip it into a compound of 90% alcohol and 10% water.

Bio-impedance [14] describes the passive electrical properties of biological materials and serves as an indirect transducing mechanism for physiological events, often in cases where no specific transducer for that event does exist. It is an elegantly simple technique that requires only the application of two or more electrodes (this is a big disadvantage of this method). The impedance between the electrodes may reflect "seasonal variations in blood flow, cardiac activity, respired volume, bladder, blood and kidney volumes, uterine contractions, nervous activity, the galvanic skin reflex, the volume of blood cells, clotting, blood pressure and salivation" [14].

4.1.8 Physical Characteristics: Pulse

Scanners based on this technique try to detect whether the scanned object exhibits characteristics of the pulse and blood flow consistent with a live human being [4, 10]. It is not very difficult to determine whether the object indicates some kind of pulse and blood flow, but it is very difficult to decide whether the acquired characteristics are coincident with a live sample. It is difficult to create an acceptance range of the sensor, which would lead to small error rates. The main problem is that the pulse of a human user varies from person to person—it depends on the emotional state of the person and also on the physical activities performed before the scanning procedure. In addition, the pulse and blood flow of the attacker's finger may be detected and accepted when a wafer-thin artificial sample is used.

The sensor usually detects variation in the levels of the reflected light energy from the scanned object as evidence of the pulse and blood flow [3, 4]. First, the light source illuminates in infrared the object and then a photodetector measures the light energy reflected from the object. Finally, there is the processing instrument (this also controls the light source) which processes the output from the photodetector. Since there are some ways how to simulate pulse and blood flow characteristics (e.g., by flashing the light or by motion of the scanned object), scanners should have a deception detection unit [10].

4.1.9 Physiological Basics of Heart Activity

Heart activity measurements are well known as electrocardiogram (ECG) in medicine. In [4], two approaches for measuring of fine movements of papillary lines, based on optical principles, are suggested. The first solution is based on a close-up view of the fingertip acquired with a camera; the second one is distance measurement with a laser sensor. It should be noted that adding the proposed anti-spoof detection solution (either camera or laser based) to a fingerprint recognition system may significantly influence the hardware requirements imposed on the complete system. Both solutions measure the fine movements of skin on a fingertip caused by heart activity (blood circulation in a cardiovascular system), i.e., volume changes in arteries and veins.

4.1.10 Physical Characteristics: Blood Oxygenation

Sensors which measure blood oxygenation [10] are mainly used in medicine (oximeters) and have also been proposed for use in anti-spoof testing modules. The technology involves two physical principles. First, the absorption of light having two different wavelengths by hemoglobin differs depending on the degree of hemoglobin oxygenation. The sensor for the measurement of this physical characteristic contains two LEDs: one emits visible red light (660 nm) and the other infrared light (940 nm). When passing through the tissue, the emitted light is partially absorbed by blood depending on the concentration of oxygen bound on hemoglobin. Second, as the volume of arterial blood changes with each pulse, the light signal obtained by a photodetector has a pulsatile component which can be exploited for the measurement of pulse rate.

4.1.11 Fingerprint Spoof Preparation

Nowadays, it is well known that there do exist many various materials, which could be used for production of fingerprint fakes [3].

The whole process of creation of the fingerprint fakes can be divided into several categories according to input data that are available. Usually, we do not have the possibility of cooperation with the user and simultaneously we have to create a mold indirectly using another information. This method is very popularized by films but we need a little bit of "cooperation" from a genuine user.

Other methods suppose that we have an access to a sensor that we want to deceive. It is possible to either use fingerprint reactivation or fingerprint synthesis [8]. The first method is based on reactivation of a fingerprint, which remains on the sensor, using for example our breath. The second method gets fingerprint image by reconstruction from enrolled template in the biometric database.

The planned procedure of making fakes using manufactured mold and chosen material is described below. First of all the mold (we used a printed circuit board) has to be cleaned—the best way appeared to be a common toothbrush and tooth paste. After cleaning the CH14 separator is applied. When the applied separator becomes dry (approx. after 10 min, i.e., the white film can be observed), it is possible to continue. A sufficient amount of silicon is placed into a measuring glass. Optionally, a small amount of body tone paint or grated graphite powder is added. In that case the silicon mixture has to be stirred thoroughly. This mixture is then spread on the mold and pushed with spatula in order to get rid of as many air bubbles as possible. When the silicon mixture gets dry, we can remove it from the mold. The removing is performed from one chosen mold side by slowly pulling. Due to the usage of CH14 separator, the dried silicon mixture does not tear apart and it is not glued to the mold (see Fig. 4.5).

Generally, we are using over 30 various materials for preparation of a fingerprint spoof, i.e., gelatin, aspic, gummy bears, aquarium silicone (black, white, skin color), epoxy resin (CHS 1200, L285, Hobbyking), latex, etc. Some of these

Fig. 4.5 Removing dried mixture from the mold

materials are mixed with skin color or graphite, as mentioned before, because we need skin color for optical sensor or conductivity for capacitive sensors. Using these materials in combination with other advanced methods, we are able to deceive many of fingerprint sensors, incl. those ones with built-in anti-spoof mechanism.

4.2 Skin Diseases

The skin is one of the largest organs in the body, having a surface area of 1.8 m^2 and making up to 12–15% of an adult's body weight. It consists of three layers (see Fig. 4.6) [7]: *epidermis* (the outer layer), *dermis* ("true skin") and *subcutaneous* (fatty) *layer*. Structure and thickness of the skin vary with site (e.g., thick epidermis on palms and soles due to mechanical protection—up to 1.4 mm).

Skin diseases represent very important, but often neglected factor of the fingerprint acquirement. It is not possible to say in general how many people suffer from skin diseases, because there are so many various skin diseases [8, 20]. In a general, medical practice about 20–25% of patients with skin complaints are referred. When discussing whether the fingerprint recognition technology is a perfect solution capable to resolve all our security problems, we should always keep in mind those potential users who suffer from some skin disease.

The situation after successful recovery of a potential user from such skin diseases is, however, very important for the possible further use of fingerprint recognition devices. If the disease has attacked and destroyed the structure of papillary lines in the epidermis and underlying dermis (so-called dermoepidermal junction—connection of the top two layers of the skin), the papillary lines will not grow in the same form as before (if at all) and therefore this user could be restricted in his future life by being excluded from the use of fingerprint recognition systems, though his fingers do not have any symptoms of the skin disease anymore.

Skin is constantly being regenerated. A keratinocyte ("skin cell") starts its life at the lower layer of epidermis (the basal layer), which is nourished by blood vessels and is supplied with nerve endings from dermis. The cell migrates upward from basal layer to stratum corneum (the outermost skin layer). During 4 weeks the cell undergoes a series of changes, gradually flattening out and moving toward the surface. Then it dies and is shed. This physiological process can be negatively affected in many diseases of the skin. The epidermis is not supplied with blood vessels, but has nerve endings. The shape of dermoepidermal junction basically forms the structure of papillary lines.

In the most cases of dermatological disorders we find a lot of changes in the ultrastructure of the skin, including epidermis and dermis. There is often inflammation (inflammatory cells), atrophy or hypertrophy, fibrotisation and many other changes visible in the microscope. These differences result in changes of color (optical characteristics), changes of dermal vessels and capillaries (blood perfusion), changes of elasticity, and thickness of the skin (optical characteristics after pressure change).

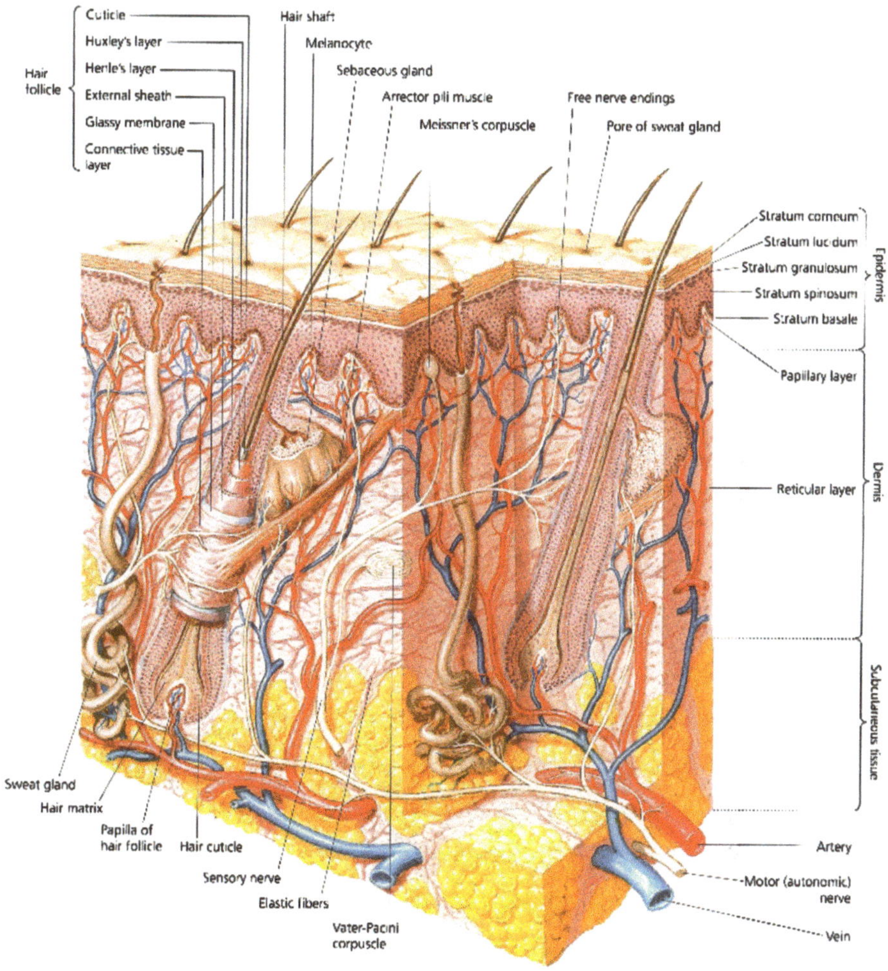

Fig. 4.6 Skin structure [7]

Diseases Causing Histopathological Changes of Epidermis and Dermis
These diseases usually cause problems for all kinds of fingerprint scanners, because they can influence either color or internal structure of the skin.

The most common representatives of this group are [7, 20]: *Hand and fingertip eczema*, *Dyshidrosis*, *Tinea*, *Pyoderma*, *Pitted keratolysis*, *Pyogenic granuloma*, *Systemic sclerosis*, or *Raynaud's phenomenon*.

Diseases Causing Skin Discoloration
These diseases may cause problems for optical fingerprint scanners and also for scanners which use a fingerprint anti-spoof detection check based on the color or spectral analysis of the human skin.

Typical representatives are [7, 20]: *Macular drug eruptions and rashes in infectious diseases (Hand, foot and mouth disease, Scarlet fever, Secondary syphilis, Kawasaki's disease), Pitted keratolysis, Raynaud's phenomenon, Xanthomas, Carotenosis,* or *Hereditary hemorrhagic teleangiectasia.*

Diseases Causing Histopathological Changes in Junction of Epidermis and Dermis

These diseases could cause structure changes underneath the skin in the junction between dermis and epidermis, i.e., in the area from that ultrasonic fingerprint

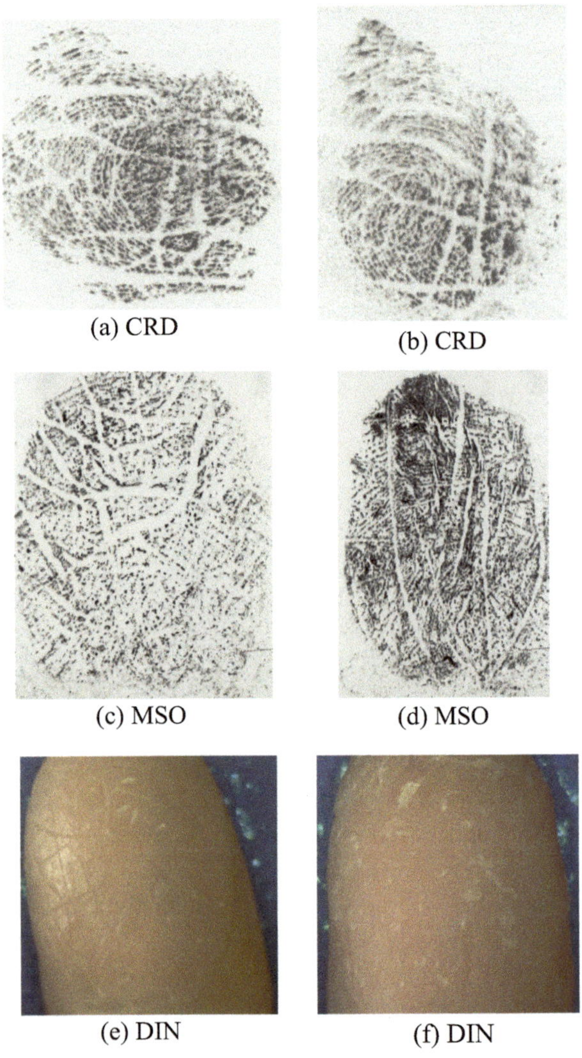

Fig. 4.7 Fingertip eczema—a severe form

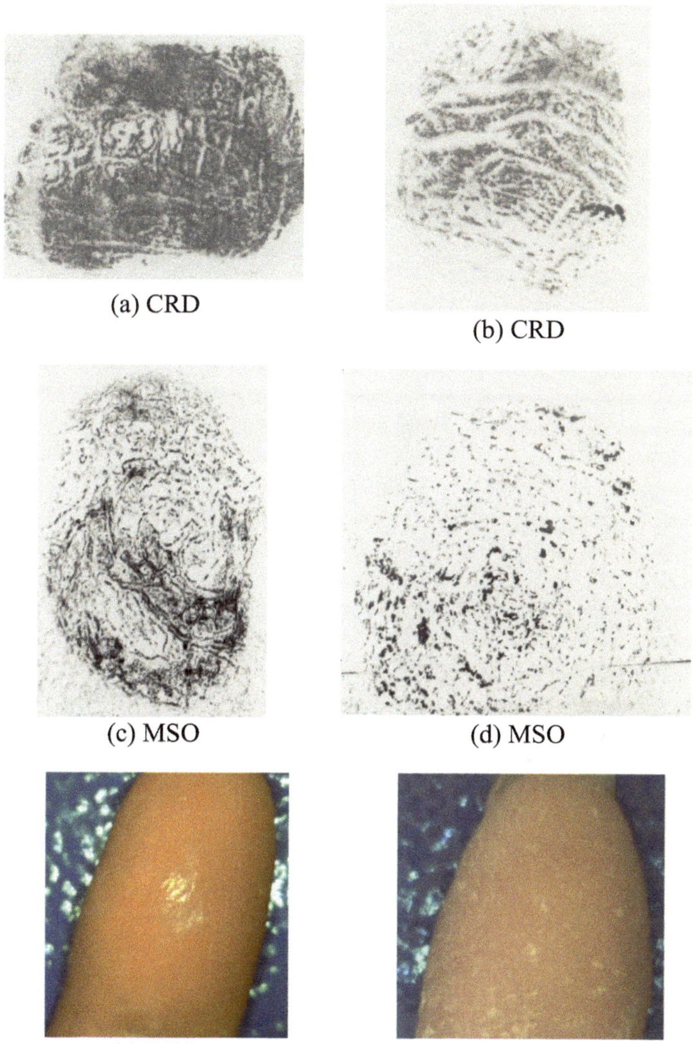

(a) CRD (b) CRD

(c) MSO (d) MSO

(e) DIN (f) DIN

Fig. 4.8 Psoriasis—a full seizure

scanners acquire fingerprint pattern images. Typical representatives are [7, 20]: *Hand eczema*, *Verruca vulgaris* (*warts*), *Psoriasis*, or *Epidermolysis bullosa*.

In the following section, examples (Figs. 4.7, 4.8, 4.9 and 4.10) of results of disease-affected fingerprint data collection are shown. The name of the disease and description are given in each figure heading. The codename of applied capturing

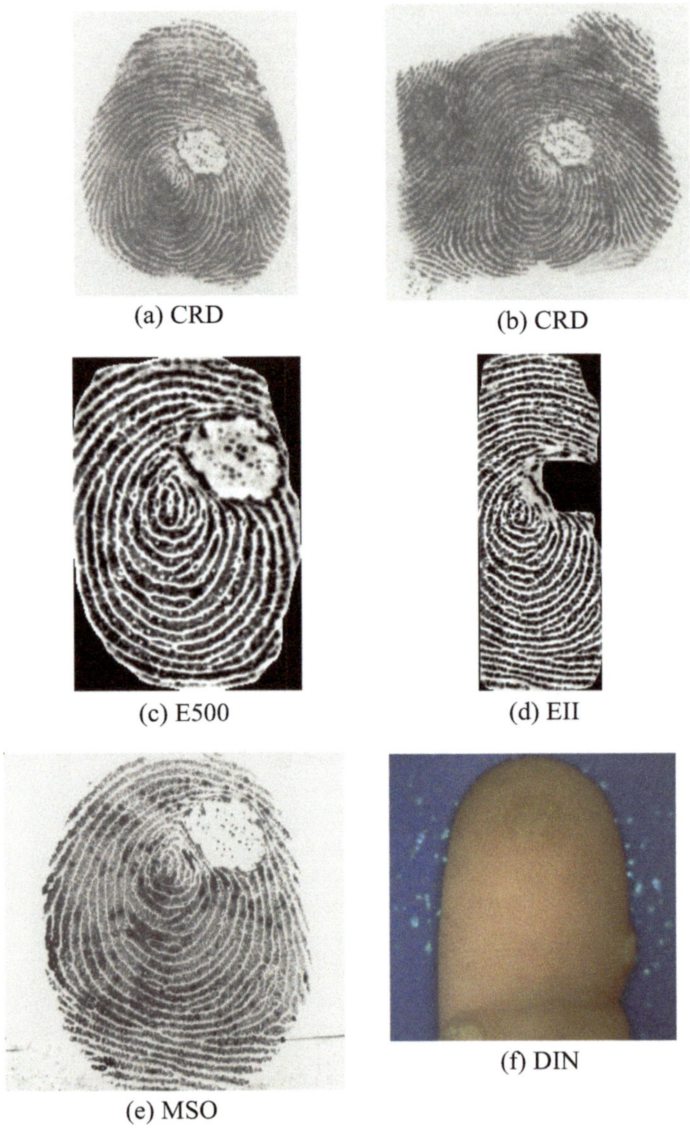

(a) CRD (b) CRD (c) E500 (d) EII (e) MSO (f) DIN

Fig. 4.9 Verruca vulgaris (wart)

principle is stated under each subfigure. We use the following codenames: CRD (dactyloscopic card), MSO (Sagem MSO 300), E500 (UPEK EikonTouch500), EII (UPEK Eikon II), TBS (TBS 3D Enroll 2011), and DIN (Dinolite).

Fig. 4.10 Colagenosis

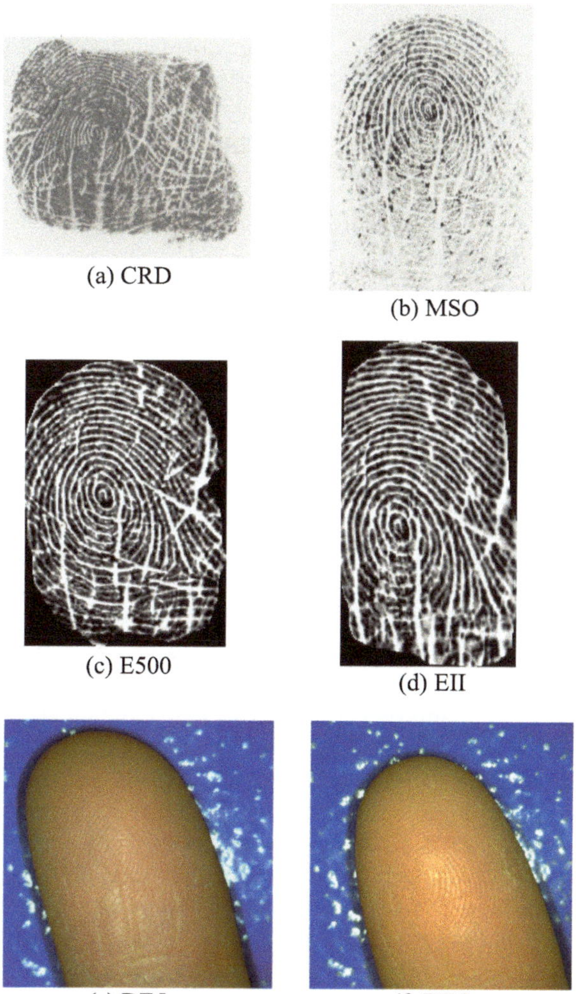

(a) CRD (b) MSO (c) E500 (d) EII (e) DIN (f) DIN

4.3 Environmental Distortions

When we finally place finger in the acquisition area there are still some difficulties. Environment around us is not ideal like in laboratory—so there are some influencing factors. We can divide them into three categories: *finger condition*, *sensor condition*, and *environment itself*. Some of these factors can be prevented but only with full support of users and thorough care of the sensor and specialized room. As you can see it is not possible to fully prevent all these factors. Consequently, sensors and recognition algorithms have to be prepared for this situation. The only way how to prepare them is by using large test dataset of damaged fingerprints. Unfortunately such data is not usually available. But we can create this data artificially. These topics are covered in the following subsections, first factors that influence resulting fingerprint are discussed, followed by creation of artificial fingerprints.

4.3.1 Phenomena Influencing Fingerprint Acquisition

As was mentioned before we can divide these factors into three groups: *user condition, sensor condition,* and *environment*—these factors will be discussed next. Each of these factors is described with example and sensor technologies that are influenced more or technologies that are not influenced at all.

First user condition is a *dirt on the finger*—it could be a small particle, a few grains of dust, or just a greasy finger. Conductive materials and liquids are usually the most problematic types of dirt. Only ultrasonic, contactless, and e-field technologies are resistant against this type of damage. *Dry or moist finger* is one of the most typical cases of damage done to a fingerprint. This is caused because we wash our hands or we are nervous and our fingers are getting sweat or on the other hand we have very dry hands because of some lotion, our skin resistance can increase or decrease ten times to the normal value. This plays usually a huge role in the recognition by optical, capacitive, and e-field sensors. *Physical damage* of a finger like cuts or abrasions is obviously damaging the fingerprint. If it is not a deep injury that influences papillary lines forever, the ultrasonic and e-field technologies scan the finger in the deeper dermis layer where the fingerprint keeps undamaged. Another factor is *skin diseases* which were thoroughly described in the previous subchapter. *Pressure and skin plasticity* can turn the fingerprint into a big black oval. Only contactless sensors are fully immune to the damage that the pressure can make. The change of pressure, very big or very low pressure or moving of the finger is also considered being part of the next category that is *non-cooperative behavior.* The user usually uses an unexpected pressure, moves when the device is scanning and/or places the finger in a wrong place or with a wrong rotation. None of the technologies is fully resistant to these types of behavior [3, 9].

The second group of factors is connected to the sensor. *Dirt on the surface* has the same effects like the dirt on the finger. The problem is that it is affecting everyone who is using this device. It means that in the registration phase this factor can create a common error for every user and there is a danger that these users will not be able to be identified after cleaning up the device. In addition to fingers there are more types of dirt than can pollute the sensor area: for example metallic dust, wooden dust, earth dust, fine sand, excrements (in outdoor use). In addition to ultrasonic and e-field technologies, every sweep sensor is also more resistant to this type of damage. *Latent fingerprint* is closely related to the previous topic. It is in some way a type of dirt on the surface of the sensor. More than damaging a new fingerprint there is a security hazard. The technologies, which are resistant to latent fingerprint, are the same like those in the previous topic. *Sensor technology* itself determines how the fingerprint will look like. Some technologies support only binary images or use specific pallet of colors to represent ridges and valleys, some can create 3D maps. *Physical damage* is an extreme but a possible influencing factor of the resulting fingerprint. There is no easy way to prevent the sensor from damaging. The damage of the sensor will have various effects on every technology [3, 9].

Finally, the surrounding environment itself will be discussed. *Vibration* can break down the sensor and slightly change the position of a finger. Only sensors using the sweep technology are, to a certain degree, resistant to this type of damage. *Temperature* can be different for the sensor, the finger or the environment. Typically, there are no problems with the exception of the thermal technology. But when we think about extreme temperatures, we have to deal with very dry or very moist fingers which can affect the resulting image. Also it is known that the ultrasonic technology does not operate properly in extremely low temperatures. *Surrounding light* is only affecting optical and electrooptical technologies because they have a light sensing unit. When the sensor area is larger or the finger of the user is smaller or the contactless technology is used, the influence of the surrounding light can be huge. *Electromagnetic radiation* is an influencing factor which affects every technology. The device as a whole can be influenced by electromagnetic radiation. Wires inside or outside connecting it to other parts of a biometric system and all electronic components can be influenced [3, 9].

4.3.2 Methods for Generation of Synthetic Fingerprints

The synthetic fingerprint generation is an inverse biometrics problem. According to input variables we basically do the fingerprint recognition process from the end to the start. There are several methods how to generate a synthetic fingerprint. When we thoroughly study them, we can find that they are all based on the same principle. The method used by the SFinGe seems to be the oldest one and also the most commonly known so it will be described as a pattern for others.

For better understanding we can look at the upper part of Fig. 4.11 to see the process of the generation. Firstly, the fingerprint shape is determined. The basic shape is oval and each elliptical segment can be changed to create the required shape. The second step is the directional field model. In this step, the fingerprint class is chosen and together with that the position of cores and deltas. This step is using the Sherlock and Monroe ridge [12] flow model to generate a consistent directional field. The third step creates the density map. When we look at a fingerprint, we can find that the density of papillary lines is not the same throughout the whole area. After examining several real fingerprints some heuristic criteria could be made. These criteria are based on the position of singularities (cores and deltas) and according to them the density map is generated. The last step is ridge pattern generating. This phase uses all previous steps and some initial seeds. Iteratively, the image with initial seeds is refined with the Gabor filter. The filter

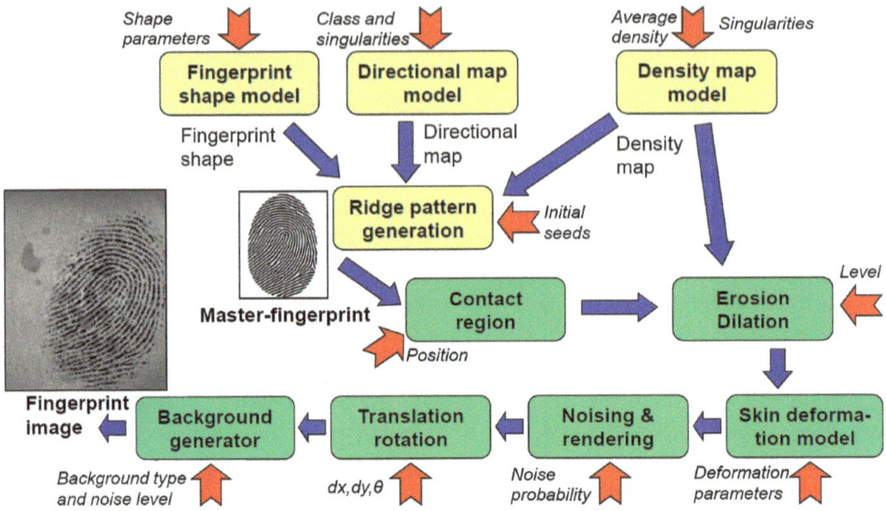

Fig. 4.11 SFinGe process of artificial fingerprint generation

orientation and frequency is adjusted according to the directional field and density map. Minutiae are automatically generated at random places with random types that are not only ridge ending and bifurcation, but also more complex ones. After that phase, the fingerprint is done [9, 12, 21].

As we can see, the SFinGe[1] generating process is not exactly an inverted recognition process. When we strictly follow this process, we do the so-called fingerprint reconstruction. These are the methods that focus on the creation of the whole fingerprint only from minutiae saved as a template in fingerprint recognition. Another method is somewhere between these two. It says that fingerprint features are dependent on each other. It is following the same scheme but with dependencies on other steps. The orientation field is influenced by singular points. The minutiae density is higher around singularities and also their appearance is not random but it is statistically driven. The minutiae direction is also dependent on their types and on the orientation of ridges around. This method firstly determines singular points, after that the orientation field and lastly the minutiae. Each step is dependent on the previous one. After all the steps the fingerprint is made with the use of the AM-FM method [21].

The last method uses minutiae as an input. The creation of the whole fingerprint is based only on these minutiae. The biggest difference is that the orientation field is generated from minutiae and not from classes or singular points as it was in the previous methods. It is generated from the minutiae direction and each minutia has a weight based on the distance of it from the point where we are determining the orientation field. The disadvantage of this method is that the final fingerprint could

[1]http://biolab.csr.unibo.it/sfinge.html.

have a class that does not exist in the real world. The density map can be manually changed in this method. After that, using a similar method of Gabor filter like in SFinGe, master fingerprint is generated. Note that instead of initial seeds, this method uses minutiae as these seeds and the generation start with them so the precisely defined minutiae don't change in the process of generation [9].

To sum it up, we can create these artificial fingerprints from ISO template, based on statistical values, using random seeds and random minutiae points or using fixed minutiae points. For testing random fingerprints is this usually fully sufficient. All these methods end with creation of the artificial fingerprint which is called master fingerprint. This master fingerprint is what was mentioned at the start of this chapter that is perfect finger perfectly scanned with no influence of the environment.

To create more realistic fingerprint we have to add these influential factors. It is time to look at the lower part of the Fig. 4.11. There are certain damage simulation methods. The first step is the selection of the contact region. To simulate the different placements of the finger on the sensor area a random translation of the ridge pattern is made. The next step is the variation in ridge thickness. The ridge thickness is modified to simulate various skin dampness and finger pressure. The next phase is the fingerprint distortion. In this phase, the skin deformation according to different finger placements over the sensor is simulated. The skin plasticity (compression or stretching) and a different force applied on each part of the finger creates a nonlinear distortion. The next step is noising and rendering. Another phase is the global translation or rotation. This phase simulates the not perfectly placed finger on the sensor. So it slightly translates and/or rotates the whole image. The last step is the generation of a realistic background. The background is generated randomly from a set of background images. At the end of that step, the fingerprint impression is made [9, 12, 21].

Please note that SFinGe system, which was used here as an example of generation and damaging of the artificial fingerprint, lies the focus in realistic looking fingerprints without exact simulation of the damage done to the fingerprint. Some steps clearly simulate specific damage, others are used as an appropriation of several factors, which is to some extent sufficient but when we want to create fingerprints acquired in some extreme environment or one which is often and more severely influenced by some phenomena we have to use precise damage simulations. We work on these damage simulations (incl. skin diseases) at the moment.

4.4 Conclusion

At the beginning of this chapter, there are described anti-spoofing methods, which are used for liveness detection on fingers in general. Some relevant advantages and disadvantages of these methods are discussed as well. Furthermore, the second part includes description of skin diseases on fingers influencing the fingerprint recognition process. It has to be noted that the anti-spoofing methods have big troubles with diseased fingers, because these fingers are very often falsely evaluated as nonliving (fake fingers). Therefore, it is very important to implement appropriate methods for anti-spoofing, which can handle diseased fingers. The last part of this chapter is devoted to other environmental influencing factors, which can cause troubles in the process of fingerprint recognition. These factors have similar impact as diseased fingers, i.e. there could be seen comparable impact to the fingerprint recognition process. As mentioned before, it is very important to find a good and reliable method for anti-spoofing, which can correctly treat diseased fingers or acquired fingerprints by various influencing factors coming from the environment.

Acknowledgments This work was supported by The Ministry of Education, Youth and Sports of the Czech Republic from the National Programme of Sustainability (NPU II); project "IT4Innovations excellence in science"—LQ1602; "New solutions for multimodal biometrics—enhancement of security and reliability of biometric technologies"—COST LD14013 (CZ); "Reliability and Security in IT"—internal Brno University of Technology project FIT-S-14-2486 (CZ).

References

1. Ambalakat P (2005) Security of biometric authentication systems. In: 21st Computer Science Seminar, SA1-T1-1 (2005), p 7
2. Daugman J (2001) Biometric Decision Landscapes, University of Cambridge, p 13
3. Drahanský M (2011) Fingerprint Recognition Technology—Related Topics. Saarbrücken, DE, LAP, 2011, p 172. ISBN 978-3-8443-3007-6
4. Drahanský M, Funk W, Nötzel R (2006) Liveness detection based on fine movements of the fingertip surface. In: IEEE—The West point workshop, West Point, New York, USA, pp 42–47. ISBN 1-4244-0130-5
5. Drahanský M, Hejtmánková D (2010) New experiments with optical liveness testing methods. J Inf Hiding Multimedia Signal Process 1(4):301–309. ISSN 2073-4212
6. Habif TP (2004) Clinical dermatology, 4th edn. Mosby, China, p 1004. ISBN 978-0-323-01319-2
7. Habif TP (2004) Clinical dermatology, 4th edn. Mosby, China, p 1004. ISBN 978-0-323-01319-2
8. Jain AK, Flynn P, Ross AA (2008) Handbook of biometrics. Springer, p 556. ISBN 978-0-387-71040-2
9. Kanich O (2014) Fingerprint damage simulation—A simulation of fingerprint distortion, damaged sensor, pressure and moisture, LAP LAMBERT Academic Publishing GmbH & Co. KG, p 57. ISBN 978-3-659-63942-5
10. Kluz M (2005) Liveness testing in biometric systems. Master Thesis, Faculty of Informatics, Masaryk University Brno, CZ, p 57
11. Lodrová D (2013) Security of biometric systems. Dissertation thesis, FIT BUT, Brno (CZ), p 152
12. Maltoni D, Maio D, Jain AK, Prabhakar S (2009) Handbook of fingerprint recognition, 2nd edn. Springer, p 494. ISBN 978-1-84882-253-5
13. Malý T (2013) Detekce živosti prstu pomocí osvětlení různé vlnové délky (Detection of Finger Liveness using Illumination with Different Wavelengths), Diploma thesis, FIT BUT, Brno (CZ), p 59
14. Martinsen ØG, Grimnes S, Haug E (1999) Measuring depth depends on frequency in electrical skin impedance measurements. In: Skin research and technology, No. 5, pp 179 –181. ISSN 0909-752X

15. Matsumoto T, Matsumoto H, Yamada K, Hoshino S (2005) Impact of artificial "Gummy" fingers on fingerprint systems. In: Proceedings of SPIE, Optical Security and Counterfeit Deterrence Techniques IV, vol 4677, p 11
16. Rowe RK (2008) Spoof Detection. Summer school for advanced studies on biometrics for secure authentication. Italy, Alghero, p 43
17. Schuckers S, Hornak L, Norman T, Derakhshani R, Parthasaradhi S (2003) Issues for liveness detection in biometrics. West Virginia University, Presentation, CITeR, p 25
18. Tan B, Lewicke A, Schuckers S (2008) Novel methods for fingerprint image analysis detect fake fingers. In: SPIE, p 3. doi:10.1117/2.1200805.1171
19. Organism Identifying Method and Device. US Patent 6,314,195, Nov 2001
20. Wolff K, Johnson RA, Suurmond D (2005) Fitzpatrick's Color Atlas and Synopsis of Clinical Dermatology, 5th Edition. McGraw-Hill, USA, p 1085. ISBN 0-07-144019-4
21. Zhao Q, Jain AK, Paulter NG, Taylor M (2012) Fingerprint image synthesis based on statistical feature models. In: 2012 IEEE Fifth International Conference on Biometrics: Theory, Applications and Systems (BTAS). IEEE, pp 23–30

Chapter 5
Altered Fingerprint Detection

John Ellingsgaard and Christoph Busch

Abstract The success of Automated Fingerprint Identification Systems (AFIS) has lead to an increased number of incidents where individuals alter their fingerprints in order to evade identification. This is especially seen at border crossings where fingerprints are subject to comparison against a watch list. This chapter discusses methods for automatically detecting altered fingerprints. The methods are based on analyses of two different local characteristics of a fingerprint image. The first analysis identifies irregularities in the pixel-wise orientations which share similar characteristics to singular point. The second analysis compares minutia orientations covering a local, but larger area than the first analysis. A global density map is created in each of the analysis in order to identify the distribution of the analyzed discrepancies. Experimental results suggest that the method yields performance fully comparable to the current state-of-the-art method. Further improvements can be achieved by combining the most efficient analysis of the two methods. The promising results achieved in this study are attractive for further investigations. Especially, studies into the possibility of introducing alteration detection into standard quality measures of fingerprints which would improve AFIS and contribute to the fight against fraud.

5.1 Introduction

Identification using fingerprints is the most matured and widespread biometric technique that currently exists. Fingerprints have a long history as a tool for identification and forensic purposes. Technological advancement has lead to the development

J. Ellingsgaard
Technical University of Denmark, Anker Engelunds Vej 1, 2800
Kongens Lyngby, Denmark
e-mail: jellingsgaard@hotmail.com

C. Busch (✉)
Norwegian Biometrics Laboratory, Norwegian University of Science
and Technology (NTNU), P.O. Box 191, 2802 Gjøvik, Norway
e-mail: christoph.busch@ntnu.no

M. Tistarelli and C. Champod (eds.), *Handbook of Biometrics for Forensic Science*, Advances in Computer Vision and Pattern Recognition,
DOI 10.1007/978-3-319-50673-9_5

of Automated Fingerprint Identification Systems (AFIS), which are used by border control and law enforcement agencies for identification purposes.

One such application is the European Visa Information System (VIS). The system consists of distributed national interfaces (NI-VIS) that are linked together with a central information system (CS-VIS) [8]. The system contains alphanumeric data as well as biometric data in the form of fingerprints and photographs, for identification and verification purposes. One method used to avoid identification of such a system is to alter one's fingerprints e.g. by obfuscating ridge flows by scraping, cutting or burning, or even in extreme measures using plastic surgery [43].

Altered fingerprints on a real finger are not necessarily easy to spot by a quick glance on the fingers of a data subject. Changes can be subtle to the naked eye and would require officers to do a closer inspection of every finger to positively identify alterations. The international standard ISO/IEC 30107-1 [18] defines a presentation attack instrument (PAI) as the biometric characteristic or object used in a sensor-based presentation attack. Artificial (fake) or human-based characteristics are the two main categories; a third category covering natural cases such as animal- and plant-based PAI is also included for completeness. Figure 5.1 gives an overview of presentation attack types while examples of each of the types belonging to the two main categories are shown in Table 5.1.

This chapter will deal with the aspect of detecting altered fingerprints. The objective is not to identify the actual identity of an individual that has altered fingerprints,

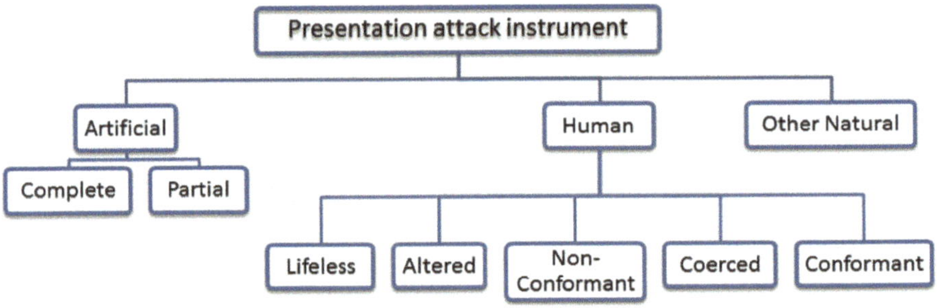

Fig. 5.1 Types of presentation attacks. *Source* [ISO-IEC 30107-1]

Table 5.1 Artificial and human attack presentation characteristics [18]

Main	Characteristic	Example
Artificial	Complete	Gummy finger
	Partial	Glue on finger
Human	Lifeless	Cadaver part, severed finger/hand
	Altered	Mutilation, surgical switching of fingerprints
	Non-Conformant	Tip or side of finger
	Coerced	Unconscious, under duress
	Conformant	Zero effort impostor attempt

but instead to detect and raise an alarm if a fingerprint is considered to be altered. The chapter is structurally divided into four parts. The first part introduces the history of altered fingerprints. The second part describes related work and state-of-the-art algorithms for detecting altered fingerprints. The third part is the contribution of a proposed algorithm for detecting altered fingerprints. Finally the results are evaluated and discussed.

5.2 Background of Fingerprint Alterations

Fingerprints have a long history of being used for forensics and other identification purposes. As the importance of the usage of fingerprints has grown through time and identification techniques have improved, the instances of individuals trying to deceive the system and avoid being identified have become more common. Already back in 1935 H. Cummins [9] published information on three criminal cases involving altered fingerprints. The cases were among others the following:

- John Dillinger applied acid to the finger tips in order to burn and permanently change the fingerprints. After his death it was determined that careful examination of the remaining undamaged areas of the fingerprints would be enough to positively identify him solely on the fingerprints.
- Gus Winkler mutilated four of his fingerprints on the left hand, excluding the thumb, possibly by the combination of slashing and deeply scraping. He was actually successful in changing his pattern type from double loop to left loop (see Fig. 5.2).

Other incidents demonstrate individuals using more advanced and inventive techniques for masquerading their identity.

- Robert J. Philipps (1941) attempted to completely erase his fingerprints by transplanting skin grafted from the side of his chest onto the fingertips [16].
- Jose Izquierdo (1997) cut a "Z" shaped cut (see Fig. 5.3) on his fingertip and exchanged the two flaps of skin. After manually reconstructing his real fingerprint images officials managed to reveal his true identity; this came with a large cost of approximately 170 h of manual and computer searching [41].

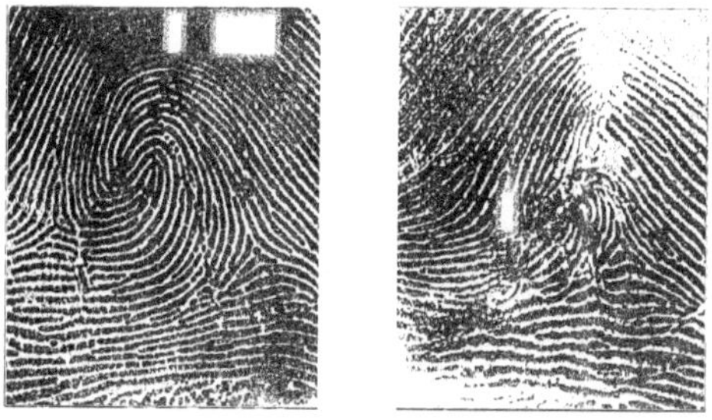

(a) Before mutilation (b) After mutilation

Fig. 5.2 Gus Winkler changed the pattern type from double loop to left loop. *Source* [9]

(a) Before z-cut (b) After z-cut (c) Before z-cut (d) After z-cut

Fig. 5.3 Illustrations of how two flaps of skin can be exchanges within a "Z" shaped cut. The numbers and colors are merely for illustration purposes to show skin positions before and after the surgery. Altered fingerprints using a "Z" shaped cut in the skin [41]

Fig. 5.4 Images of altered fingertips [22]

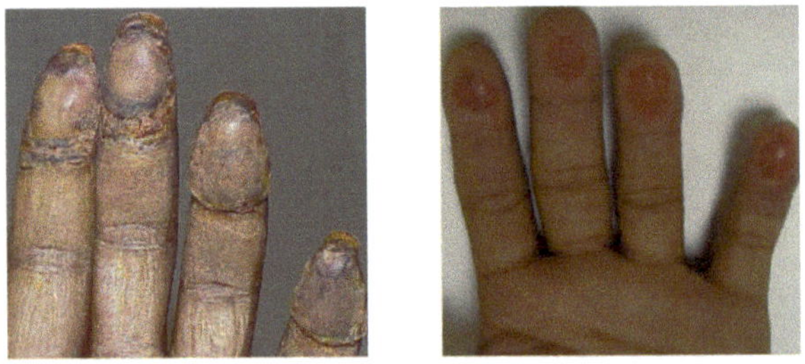

(a) Skin transplanted from sole of foot (b) Bitten fingertips

The above mentioned examples are examples from forensic investigations. However, border crossings are seeing an increased amount of asylum seekers and migrants with mutilated fingerprints who try to avoid being identified. The *MailOnline* reported on migrants mutilating their fingertips to hide their identity [29]. Images that show actual fingers with altered fingertips can be seen in Fig. 5.4.

Based on the observations by Feng [13] altered fingerprints are classified into three categories based on the changes in ridge pattern due to alteration [43]. The classification types are based on the fingerprint image and not on the actual alteration process [44]. The following will describe these categories, analyze discrepancies, and special features of fingerprints in these categories, which will serve as the basis for understanding the structure of common alterations.

5.2.1 Obliteration

Probably the most common form of alteration is *obliteration*, which relates to diminishing or even destroying the quality of the friction ridge patterns on the fingertips in order to make it problematic to match with the enroled reference. Obliteration can be performed by incision, scraping, burning, applying acids or transplanting smooth

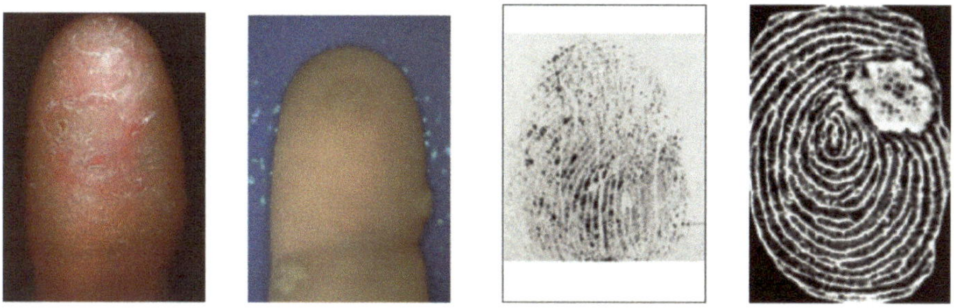

(a) Finger eczema (b) Wart (c) Finger eczema (d) Wart

Fig. 5.5 Diseases can obliterate a fingerprint. Images and subsequent fingerprint images do not belong to the same subjects. *Source* [10]

skin [13]. John Dillinger for instance mutilated his fingertips with acids. Obliteration can be perceived as a natural extension to the problem of identifying low quality fingerprints [34]. The quality of unaltered fingerprints can vary depending on different factors such as the quality of the actual scan or damages such as scars. Also skin diseases such as eczema or warts can have a degrading impact on the quality of the friction ridge patterns (see Fig. 5.5). Fingerprint quality assessment software such as NFIQ2.0 [33] could in many cases be used to deny enrolling or comparing a heavily obliterated fingerprint, since the quality would simply be deemed too low for comparison.

5.2.2 Distortion

Distortion is the reshaping of the original patterns of the friction ridges. This can be done by removing and reorganizing portions of skin from fingertips or by transplanting other skin with friction ridge patterns unto the fingertip. The resulting fingerprints on the fingertips will have unnatural ridge patterns. Jose Izquierdo distorted his fingerprints by exchanging two portions of skin on the fingertip by a "Z" shaped cut (see Fig. 5.3). Fingertips that have been successfully distorted may reach a high sample quality score [17, 32], since they will have clearly visible friction ridge patterns throughout the whole fingerprints; possibly even preserving ridge properties such as width and frequency over the entire fingerprint area. A closer look at a distorted fingerprint will however show clear irregularities. There will typically be sudden changes in the orientation of friction ridges along the scars where different skin patches are joined together. Also, distortion can result in unnatural distribution of singular points (Table 5.2).

Unaltered fingerprints normally have a smooth orientation field throughout the whole fingerprint except in the vicinity of singular points.

Table 5.2 Characteristics of distortion

	Distortion
Definition	Misrepresentation, misshape, a change in perception so that it does not correspond to reality (psychology)
Performed by	Removing and reorganizing portions of skin from fingertips or by transplanting skin with friction ridge patterns
Characteristics	Unnatural ridge patterns and scarred areas

5.2.3 Imitation

The most advanced category of altered fingerprints is imitated fingerprints. This is not referring to spoofing or artefacts as presentation attack instrument but rather to the required skills and the quality of the alteration. Imitated fingerprints have friction ridge patterns that both preserve ridge properties, e.g., width and frequency, while also containing the typical smooth orientation field pattern found in unaltered fingerprints. A typical imitation technique includes transplantation of a large area of friction ridge skin. An example is to remove a portion of friction ridge skin and thereafter join together the remaining skin. For this to be a success, friction ridges on each side of the scar must principally avoid abrupt changes in orientations. Gus Winkler was successful in this technique, even changing the type of his finger pattern in the process. The main difference between *distortion* and *imitation* is the fact that imitated fingerprints maintain the smooth orientation field characteristics of an unaltered fingerprint.

The problem with imitated fingerprints is that they contain so many properties of an unaltered fingerprint and are of such a good quality that they will successfully pass fingerprint quality assessment software. Well executed imitation can even be hard to spot even with a close inspection of the fingertips by the human expert.

The main focus of the following section is on distorted fingerprints. Obliterated fingerprints will, in most cases, already be processed correctly based on the area and amount of obliteration. Either fingerprint quality assessment software will evaluate that the fingerprint quality is too low or it will be processed correctly in the biometric identification system. Distorted fingerprints can have a high quality level and share many properties with unaltered fingerprints. However, they have clearly identifiable properties, such as irregular and abrupt changes in the orientation of friction ridges.

5.3 Related Work

Relatively limited research has been done in the field of automatically detecting altered fingerprints. Yoon [43] proposed a technique based on analyzing discontinuity and abnormality in the flow of the friction ridges along with analyzing the spatial distribution of minutiae. The algorithm is based on two different analyses.

- Analysis of the friction ridge orientations. Fingerprints generally have a smooth ridge flow except in the vicinity of a *singular point*. Altered fingerprints will typically result in irregular and abrupt changes in the ridge flow in some areas of the fingerprint. This approach tries to identify regions of unnatural ridge flow. The algorithm is called *Orientation Field Analysis (OFA)* in this chapter.
- Analysis of *minutia* distribution. A minutia point is located at local discontinuities in the fingerprint pattern where friction ridges begin, terminate or bifurcate. This analysis will be named *Minutiae Distribution Analysis (MDA)*.

Feature vectors are constructed from each of the analyses, fused into one larger feature vector and fed into a Support Vector Machine (*SVM*) for classification. The following subsections will describe how the feature vectors are constructed.

5.3.1 Orientation Field Analysis

The *Orientation Field Analysis (OFA)* uses a mathematical model for constructing an approximation of an estimated ridge flow of the fingerprint. The analysis identifies discontinuities based on differences of the ridge flow approximation and estimation, e.g. areas where the approximation is unable to correctly simulate the actual fingerprint image. The orientation of friction ridges, typically called *orientation field* and denoted θ, is defined as an image where $\theta(x, y)$ holds the estimated orientation at pixel (x, y). The steps of the analysis are the following:

1. Normalization of the image to have a common rotation and size.
2. Segmentation. The foreground of the fingerprint is separated from the background of the image in order to be able to only analyze the actual fingerprint.
3. Orientation field estimation. The $n \times n$ block-wise averaged orientation field, $\theta(x, y)$, is computed using the gradient-based method.
4. Orientation field approximation. A polynomial model is used to approximate the orientation field $\theta(x, y)$ to obtain $\hat{\theta}(x, y)$.
5. Orientation error map. The absolute difference between the orientation field $\theta(x, y)$ and the approximation $\hat{\theta}(x, y)$ is computed to yield an error map, $\epsilon(x, y)$.

Since the orientation field serves as a central part of this method and also in the upcoming proposed algorithm, a technique for constructing such an orientation field will be described in more detail.

5.3.1.1 Orientation Field Estimation

The *orientation field* is the local orientation of the friction ridges. It serves as an essential part in all stages of analyzing a fingerprint, such as preprocessing and feature extraction. The orientation field basically holds information on the local orientations of friction ridges. Orientations are typically defined in the range $[0, \pi)$. Depending on the context pixel-wise and block-wise orientation fields are used. Instead of

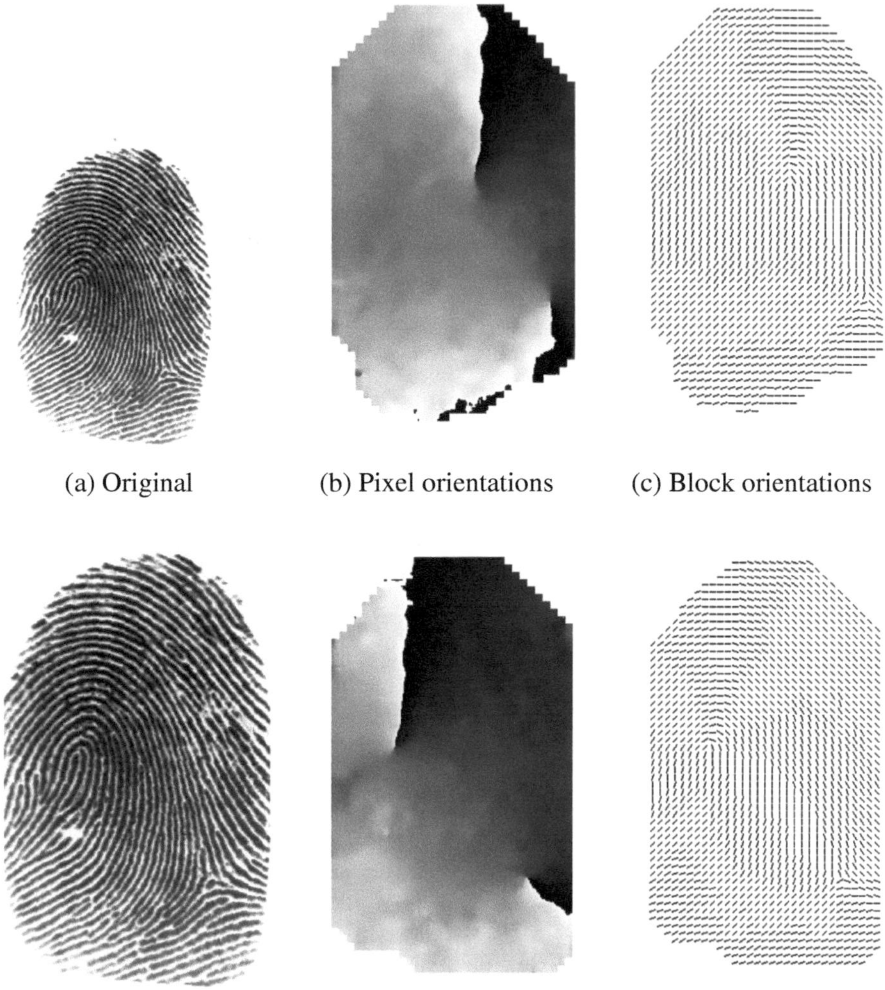

(a) Original (b) Pixel orientations (c) Block orientations

(d) Original (e) Pixel orientations (f) Block orientations

Fig. 5.6 Orientation of fingerprints. **a**, **d** show the original fingerprint images [6], **b**, **e** contain pixel-wise orientations in greyscale, and **c**, **f** show block-wise orientations

using local ridge orientation at each pixel, it is common to partition the image into smaller blocks. The block-wise orientations are derived by simply averaging the orientations within each block. Figure 5.6 shows the orientation field of two fingerprint images; the pixel-wise orientations are illustrated in greyscale while block-wise orientations use lines to represent orientations within each block.

There are two common approaches to compute the orientation field of a fingerprint: filter bank-based approaches and gradient-based approaches. An example of a filter bank-based approach is a method proposed by Kamei and Mizoguchi [24] using

Fig. 5.7 Sobel's two 3×3 gradient kernels

$$S_y = \begin{bmatrix} -1 & -2 & -1 \\ 0 & 0 & 0 \\ 1 & 2 & 1 \end{bmatrix} \quad S_x = \begin{bmatrix} -1 & 0 & 1 \\ -2 & 0 & 2 \\ -1 & 0 & 1 \end{bmatrix}$$

directional filters in the frequency domain. According to Gu and Zhou [15] filter bank-based approaches are more resistant to noise than gradient-based approaches, but computationally expensive. Gradient-based methods seems to be the most common approach for extracting local ridge orientation; probably since it is the *simplest and most natural approach* [30].

5.3.1.2 Pixel Orientation

A natural approach for extracting ridge orientation is based on computation of gradients in the fingerprint image. The first step is determining the gradient components δ_x and δ_y for each pixel in the image. This implementation uses a *Sobel* operator to define the pixel gradient components. The Sobel operator uses two 3×3 gradient filters—one for calculating the horizontal changes in the image and the other for vertical changes. The two kernels are illustrated in Fig. 5.7 where S_x is the kernel for the horizontal direction and S_y is the vertical. For each pixel, (i,j), in the image two two-dimensional convolutions with the Sobel kernels are computed, yielding the gradient components $\delta_x(i,j)$ and $\delta_y(i,j)$.

For each gradient the magnitude and vector angle can be calculated using Eqs. (5.1) and (5.2). However, pixel-wise orientation is very sensitive to noise in the fingerprint image and therefore is too detailed and somewhat inaccurate. The solution is to calculate block-wise averages of the pixel gradients.

$$G = \sqrt{{\delta_x}^2 + {\delta_y}^2} \tag{5.1}$$

$$\theta(i,j) = \frac{\pi}{2} + \arctan\left(\sqrt{\frac{\delta_x(i,j)}{\delta_y(i,j)}}\right) \tag{5.2}$$

5.3.1.3 Block-Wise Ridge Orientation

Block-wise averages of gradients have multiple purposes when processing fingerprint images. Typically the orientation (or gradients) of each pixel is first smoothed using an averaging filter from a larger area of the image before assigning block-wise orientation averages. The same averaging technique is used in both cases. Yoon et al. [43] use a 16×16 averaging filter to smoothen the pixel-wise orientations prior to computing the block-wise orientations. The equations for calculating the block-wise orientations for each block are given where pixel (i,j) is the center of the block being calculated. Equations (5.3) and (5.4) show the two components, V_x and V_y, of the doubled local ridge orientation vector [37]. W is the block size, Yoon here uses a 8×8 pixel block [43]. The dominant ridge flow is then computed according Eq. (5.5).

$$V_x(i,j) = \sum_{u=i-\frac{W}{2}}^{i+\frac{W}{2}} \sum_{v=j-\frac{W}{2}}^{j+\frac{W}{2}} 2\delta_x(u,v) \cdot \delta_y(u,v) \tag{5.3}$$

$$V_y(i,j) = \sum_{u=i-\frac{W}{2}}^{i+\frac{W}{2}} \sum_{v=j-\frac{W}{2}}^{j+\frac{W}{2}} (\delta_x(u,v)^2 - \delta_y(u,v)^2) \tag{5.4}$$

$$\theta(i,j) = \frac{\pi}{2} + \frac{1}{2} arctan2(V_y(i,j), V_x(i,j)) \tag{5.5}$$

5.3.1.4 Orientation Field Approximation

The global orientation field, $\theta(x,y)$, is approximated by a polynomial model to obtain $\hat{\theta}(x,y)$. The cosine and sine components of the doubled orientation at (x,y) can be represented by bivariate polynomials of order n:

$$g_c^n(x,y) \stackrel{\Delta}{=} \cos 2\theta(x,y) = \sum_{i=0}^{n} \sum_{j=0}^{i} a_{i,j} x^j y^{i-j} \tag{5.6}$$

$$g_s^n(x,y) \stackrel{\Delta}{=} \sin 2\theta(x,y) = \sum_{i=0}^{n} \sum_{j=0}^{i} b_{i,j} x^j y^{i-j} \tag{5.7}$$

where $a_{i,j}$ and $b_{i,j}$ are the polynomial coefficients for $g_c^n(x,y)$ and $g_s^n(x,y)$, respectively [43]. The order of the polynomial model, n, is selected to be 6. Coefficients $a_{i,j}$ and $b_{i,j}$ for the approximated polynomials $\hat{g}_c(x,y)$ and $\hat{g}_s(x,y)$, respectively, can be estimated by the least squares method. The approximated orientation field, $\hat{\theta}(x,y)$, is constructed by

$$\hat{\theta}(x,y) = \frac{1}{2} \tan^{-1}(\frac{\hat{g}_s(x,y)}{\hat{g}_c(x,y)}) \tag{5.8}$$

5.3.1.5 Orientation Error Map

Altered areas in a fingerprint, e.g. around scars and obliterated areas, can result in discontinuous or unnatural changes in the orientation field. The approximated orientation field will not be able to accurately represent these abrupt and irregular changes

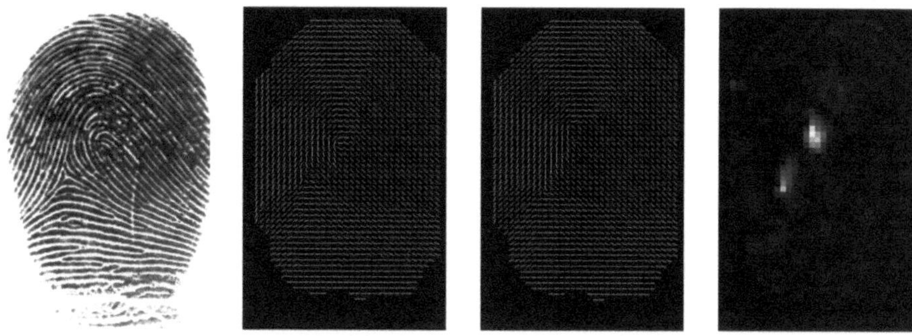

(a) Original (b) Estimation (c) Approximation (d) Error map

Fig. 5.8 *OFA* of unaltered fingerprint. The error map has high values around singularities. Source of original fingerprint image: [6]

(a) Original (b) Estimation (c) Approximation (d) Error map

Fig. 5.9 *OFA* of altered fingerprint. The approximation is unable to correctly model abrupt changes around distorted areas. The error map therefore has high values around singularities and in some scarred regions. Source of original fingerprint image: [41]

caused by alterations. An error map, $\epsilon(x, y)$, is therefore computed as the absolute difference between $\theta(x, y)$ and $\hat{\theta}(x, y)$.

$$\epsilon(x, y) = min(|\theta(x, y) - \hat{\theta}(x, y)|, \pi - |\theta(x, y) - \hat{\theta}(x, y)|)/(\pi/2) \tag{5.9}$$

The error map shows how precise the approximation is to the estimation. Abrupt changes and discontinuities in the ridge flow will result in high values in the error map. Unaltered fingerprints of good quality will therefore only have small errors around singular points, whereas altered fingerprints can additionally have errors in scarred or mutilated areas. Figures 5.8 and 5.9 illustrate the resulting orientation fields and error map of an unaltered fingerprint and an altered fingerprint, respectively.

A feature vector can be constructed from the error map in the following manner:

1. Two columns of blocks are removed from each side of the error map which results in an error map of size 60×60 blocks.
2. The error map is divided in 3×3 cells. Each cell is therefore 20×20 blocks.
3. Histograms in 21 bins in the range [0,1] are computed for each of the nine cells.
4. The nine histograms are concatenated into a 189-dimensional feature vector.

5.3.2 Minutiae Distribution Analysis

In the *Minutiae Distribution Analysis (MDA)* the minutiae extractor *MINDTCT* in NBIS [39] is used to extract minutia from a fingerprint. The analysis is based on the observation that the minutiae distribution of altered fingerprints often differs from that of natural fingerprints [43]. The analysis constructs a density map of the minutiae points by using the Parzen window method with uniform kernel function. Let $\mathbf{S_m}$ be the set of minutiae of the fingerprint, i.e.,

$$\mathbf{S_m} = \{\mathbf{x} \quad | \quad \mathbf{x} = (x, y) \text{is the position of minutia}\}. \tag{5.10}$$

The density map of the minutia is constructed as follows:

1. The initial minutia density map, $M'_d(\mathbf{x})$, is obtained by

$$M'_d(\mathbf{x}) = \sum_{\mathbf{x_0} \in \mathbf{S_m}} K_r(\mathbf{x} - \mathbf{x_0}), \tag{5.11}$$

where $K_r(\mathbf{x} - \mathbf{x_0})$ is a uniform kernel function centered at $\mathbf{x_0}$ with radius, r. Yoon [43] set the radius to 40 pixels. However, the implementation generated for study uses $r = 30$, since this gave better results.
2. The initial density map, $M'_d(x, y)$ is smoothed by a Gaussian filter (30×30 pixels) with a standard deviation of 10 pixels.
3. $M_d(x, y)$ is transformed to lie in the interval [0, 1] by

$$M_d(x, y) = \begin{cases} M'_d(x, y)/T, & \text{if } M'_d(x, y) \leq T, \\ 1, & \text{otherwise} \end{cases} \tag{5.12}$$

where T is a predetermined threshold (T is set to 6.9 in this specific implementation).

Figures 5.10 and 5.11 show the density maps of an unaltered and altered fingerprint, respectively. Alterations will cause ridge discontinuities which will result in many spurious minutiae. A feature vector is also constructed from the density map in the same fashion as for the *OFA*. 16 columns of pixels are removed from each side of the density map, resulting in an image of size 480×480 pixels. The density map is divided into 3×3 cells, where each cell is 160×160 pixels. Histograms of each cell of the density map are computed in 21 bins in the range [0, 1]. The nine histograms are concatenated to construct a 189-dimensional feature vector. The feature vector from the *OFA* is concatenated to the feature vector from the *MDA*. This results in a feature vector of 378 dimensions, which is fed into a *SVM* for classification.

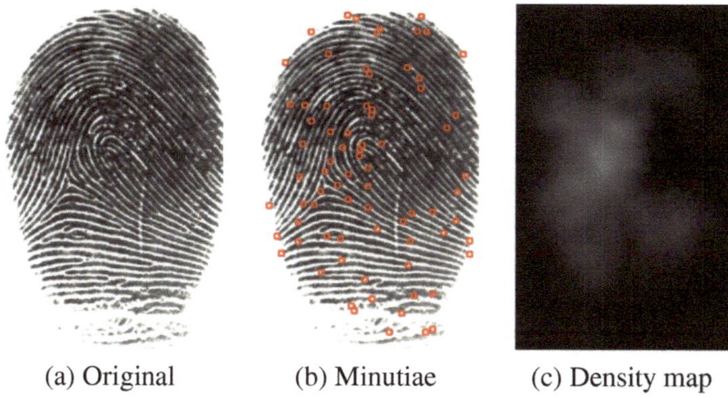

Fig. 5.10 Minutia density map of an unaltered fingerprint. Source of FP image: [6]

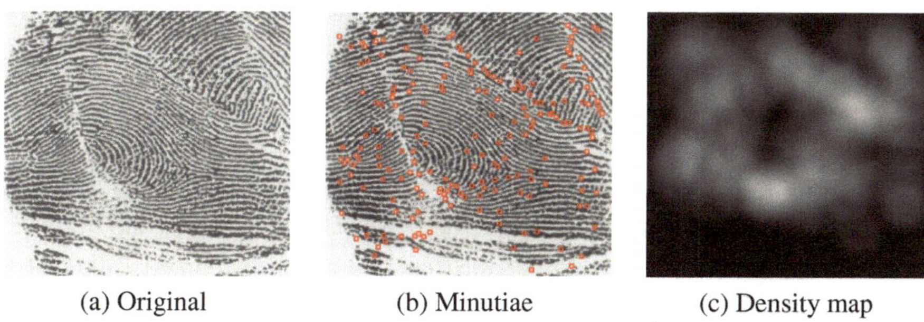

Fig. 5.11 Minutia density map of an altered fingerprint. Source of FP image: [41]

5.4 Recent Algorithms for Fingerprint Alteration Detection

Recently a new approach to detect fingerprint alterations has been proposed [12]. A rough overview of the approach is given in Fig. 5.12. The following subsections will give an introduction to the main steps of the method.

5.4.1 Preprocessing

The preprocessing pipeline is used to identify foreground and background of the image, to reduce noise and increase the contrast between ridges and valleys, and to transform the image into a common and *invariant* format. The output should thus be a fingerprint image with properties and enhancements specifically designed for the following analysis process. The pipeline consists of the following five steps:

1. Cropping. Locating and isolating the fingerprint image.
2. Segmentation. Separating the foreground from the background.

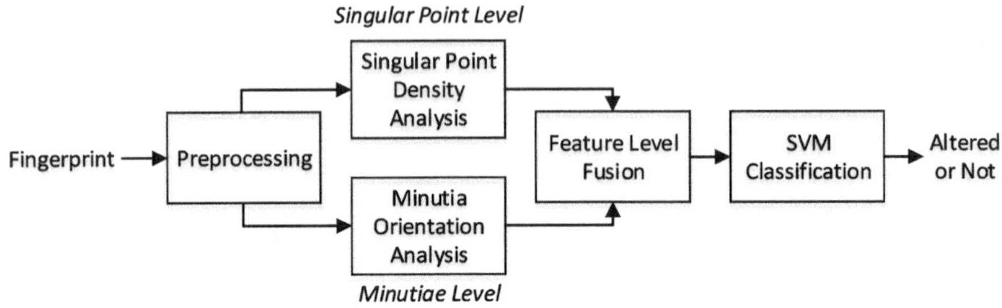

Fig. 5.12 Flowchart of the proposed algorithm

3. Rotation. Align fingerprint image along the longitudinal direction.
4. Resize. The size of the image is changed to fit a specified size.
5. Enhancement. Improve the clarity of friction ridges and minimize noise.

5.4.1.1 Cropping

The NIST NBIS package [39] includes a fingerprint segmentation algorithm, *Nfseg*, for cropping a rectangular region of an input fingerprint. As it does not align the fingerprint along the longitudinal direction, further rotation techniques will be used later in the pipeline.

5.4.1.2 Segmentation

An important image preprocessing operation is that of separating the fingerprint image ridge area (i.e., the *ROI*) from the image background. The input fingerprint image, I, is intensity normalized to have zero mean along with unit standard deviation. This is done by the following pixel-wise function:

$$\forall x \in \{1..R\}, y \in \{1..C\} \; : \; I_n(x, y) = \frac{I(x, y) - avg(I)}{std(I)} \tag{5.13}$$

where $avg(I)$ is the average pixel intensity of the input image and $std(I)$ is the standard deviation. $I(x, y)$ is the pixel intensity at pixel (x, y) of the input image. From I_n it is possible to generate a binary image, I_{mask}, known as the *mask* of the fingerprint where ones belong to the image*ROI* and zeros belong to the background. The normalized image is divided into blocks of size 8×8. If the standard deviation of a block is above a threshold, T, then the block is regarded as being part of the actual fingerprint, i.e., the foreground. This is a block-wise process; the function for creating the mask is the following: